One Pot
Favorites

The Healthy Exchanges Cookbook
HELP: The Healthy Exchanges Lifetime Plan
The Diabetic's Healthy Exchanges Cookbook
Cooking Healthy with a Man in Mind
The Best of Healthy Exchanges Food Newsletter '92 Cookbook
Notes of Encouragement
It's Not a Diet, It's a Way of Life (audiotape)

One Pot

Favorites

A HEALTHY EXCHANGES® COOKBOOK

JoAnna M. Lund

HELPing Others HELP Themselves
the **Healthy Exchanges**® Way™

A Perigee Book

A Perigee Book
Published by The Berkley Publishing Group
200 Madison Avenue
New York, NY 10016

Copyright © 1997 by Healthy Exchanges, Inc.
Diabetic Exchanges calculated by Rose Hoenig, R.D., L.D.
Book design by Jill Dinneen
Cover design and illustration by Charles Bjorklund
Front-cover photograph of the author by Glamour Shots® of West Des Moines

For more information about Healthy Exchanges products, contact:
Healthy Exchanges, Inc.
P.O. Box 124
DeWitt, Iowa 52742-0124
(319) 659-8234

Perigee Special Sales edition: January 1997
ISBN: 0-399-52324-3
Published simultaneously in Canada.

The Putnam Berkley World Wide Web site address is
http://www.berkley.com/berkley

Printed in the United States of America

10 9 8 7 6 5 4 3 2 1

Before using the recipes and advice in this book, consult your physician or health-care provider to be sure they are appropriate for you. The information in this book is not intended to take the place of any medical advice. It reflects the author's experiences, studies, research, and opinions regarding a healthy lifestyle. All material included in this publication is believed to be accurate. The publisher assumes no responsibility for any health, welfare, or subsequent damage that might be incurred from use of these materials.

This cookbook is dedicated to the staff of QVC. Am I ever glad they asked me to bring my "pot" to West Chester to cook up a storm! We've been happily cooking up those "common folk" healthy recipes together ever since.

Contents

Acknowledgments

Anyone who thinks that writing and testing three cookbooks in three months is a "piece of cake"—no matter how easy to prepare the recipes are—needs to think again! It took a lot of teamwork to get this project completed on time. For being members of the Healthy Exchanges Team, I want to thank:

John Duff and Barbara O'Shea from Putnam and Amy Rosen and Paula Piercy from QVC, for cooking up the idea in the first place.

Angela Miller and Coleen O'Shea, for assuring me I could do it.

Shirley Morrow for typing, retyping, and typing again as I changed my mind on what I wanted to include.

Rita Ahlers and Gerry Stamp, for helping me test the recipes.

Janis Jackson and Susan Williams, for doing all those dishes, and I do mean *dishes*, when well over three hundred recipes had to be tested.

Lori Hansen, for lending a hand with the Food Processor II software so the recipes could be as accurate as possible in calories and grams.

Rose Hoenig, R.D., L.D., for calculating the Diabetic Exchanges.

Barbara Alpert, for helping me get my manuscript "ready for the presses" more quickly than I could have alone.

Cliff Lund, my "Official Taste Tester." His taste buds are the "Barometer of America." If he loves it, you can bet your family, your friends, and your neighbors will love it too! And he really loves the recipes in this collection of cookbooks.

The entire Healthy Exchanges crew for giving Cliff a hand with the taste-testing responsibilities.

God, for giving me the ability to create "common folk" healthy recipes. It truly is miraculous what happens when we change our prayers from what we want to what we need.

One Pot

Favorites

How Hard Can It Be to Prepare If It's a One Pot Dish?

Over the years I've met lots of people who tell me they want to eat healthy, but they just can't do it because *they don't like to cook.* Or, they never really learned how to cook, and feel that every recipe they read is written in a foreign language. Or, they live in homes with tiny kitchens and few appliances or cooking pots. Or, it's just so much simpler to grab fast-food meals or order pizza.

Do any of these excuses sound familiar? I've heard them often, but I think I've finally figured out the answer to every one of them: a cookbook devoted solely to one pot dishes. What could be easier than that?

You'll find an astonishing variety of meals can be produced using just one cooking pot, and you can select the pot based on your needs that particular day. If you're going to be busy for hours, but long to come home to a fully cooked meal, a slow cooker recipe may fit the bill. If you walk in the door to a ravenous family and nothing planned, a speedy microwave dish will put food on the table in mere minutes. And if you don't want to use your oven because you're just cooking for yourself tonight, a quick skillet or stir-fry (rather than a call to the takeout place) is one way you can care for yourself and make a healthy choice *without* creating lots of extra cleanup.

The principle behind the recipes in this volume promises "one pot," although you may be using a few other dishes or bowls. But be assured that every "favorite" I've included has survived the test of time—that is, tested by people with little time or patience to cook complicated, multi-ingredient, five-course meals! I bet you'll use the recipes in this book again and again, because they're simple, delicious, and remarkably efficient.

Because I'm now known as the "Dessert Lady of America," I can't have a one pot cookbook that doesn't put a few dessert recipes into those pots. While the vast majority of recipes included in this collection are main dishes, you'll find a delicious selection of my special desserts, created with you in mind!

Pick your pot, choose a recipe, and you're on your way! You'll be so glad you did.

Jo Anna

Six Ways to Stir Up Successful One Pot Dishes

1. One pot dishes can be successfully stirred up in a skillet, in the oven, in the microwave, and in a slow cooker. Just be aware that more liquid is required when you simmer a dish in a skillet than when you bake it in the oven. And more liquid is required when you bake in the oven than when you use the microwave. The slow cooker requires the least liquid of all. Now that you are aware of this "cooking liquid" rule, you can start converting your traditional family recipes for the "pot of your choice."

2. Choose high-quality cookware. A good Teflon-coated skillet is essential for low-fat one pot cooking. Invest in two sturdy baking dishes—one 8-by-8-inch and one 9-by-13-inch. They ensure even baking and make portion control a snap. You'll also find that an 8-cup glass measuring bowl makes a wonderful baking dish in the microwave: it's easier to stir the contents evenly, and because the bowl is round, the chemistry of the cooking process produces an evenly cooked dish. Don't skimp when choosing a slow cooker; you'll find that you'll turn often to this appliance in years to come.

3. When a recipe calls for a preheated oven, be sure to turn the oven on at least ten minutes before you put the dish

in to bake. Just make a mental note to set the temperature of the oven *before* you reach for the mixing bowl.

4. As temperatures can vary from brand to brand and even from stove to stove, invest in an oven thermometer. If your oven temperature is hotter or colder than the oven setting, you will need to adjust your setting accordingly. Use the center shelf instead of the top shelf, as the top shelf of the oven is almost always the hottest spot. Also, realize that baking times are only suggestions, so get in the habit of checking your pot at least ten minutes before the suggested baking time ends. You can always continue to bake your dish, but you can't "unbake" it once you've left it in the oven too long.

5. In most cases, you'll be using your baking dish as a serving dish, so remember to protect your table surface by placing the pot on a trivet or wire rack. This also allows air movement under the pot and keeps the food on the bottom of your dish from getting soggy.

6. Always remember to coat your "pots" with cooking spray before adding ingredients. This makes cleanup a breeze.

JoAnna M. Lund and the Creation of Healthy Exchanges

For twenty-eight years I was the diet queen of DeWitt, Iowa. I tried every diet I ever heard of, every one I could afford, and every one that found its way to my small town in eastern Iowa. I was willing to try anything that promised to "melt off the pounds," determined to deprive my body in every possible way in order to become thin at last.

I sent away for expensive "miracle" diet pills. I starved myself on the Cambridge Diet and the Bahama Diet. I gobbled Ayds diet candies, took thyroid pills, fiber pills, prescription and over-the-counter diet pills. I went to endless weight-loss support group meetings—but I managed to turn healthy programs such as Overeaters Anonymous, Weight Watchers, and TOPS into unhealthy diets . . . diets I could never follow for more than a few months.

I was determined to discover something that worked long-term, but each new failure increased my desperation that I'd never find it.

I ate strange concoctions and rubbed on even stranger potions. I tried liquid diets like Slimfast and Metrecal. I agreed to be hypnotized. I tried reflexology and even had an acupuncture device stuck in my ear!

Does my story sound a lot like yours? I'm not surprised. No wonder the weight loss business is a billion-dollar industry!

Every new thing I tried seemed to work—at least at first. And losing that first five or ten pounds would get me so excited, I'd believe that this new miracle diet would, finally, get my weight off for keeps.

Inevitably, though, the initial excitement wore off. The diet's routine and boredom set in, and I quit. I shoved the pills to the back of the medicine chest; pushed the cans of powdered shake mix to the rear of the kitchen cabinets; slid all the program materials out of sight under my bed; and once more I felt like a failure.

Like most dieters, I quickly gained back the weight I'd lost each time, along with a few extra "souvenir" pounds that seemed always to settle around my hips. I'd done the diet-lose-weight-gain-it-all-back "yo-yo" on the average of once a year. It's no exaggeration to say that over the years I've lost 1,000 pounds—and gained back 1,150 pounds.

Finally, at the age of forty-six I weighed more than I'd ever imagined possible. I'd stopped believing that any diet could work for me. I drowned my sorrows in sacks of cake donuts, and wondered if I'd live long enough to watch my grandchildren grow up.

Something had to change.

I had to change.

Finally, I did.

I'm just over fifty now—and I'm 130 pounds less than my all-time high of close to 300 pounds. I've kept the weight off for more than six years. I'd like to lose another ten pounds, but I'm not obsessed about it. If it takes me the rest of my life to accomplish it, that's okay.

What I *do* care about is never saying hello again to any of those unwanted pounds I said good-bye to!

How did I jump off the roller coaster I was on? For one thing, I finally stopped looking to food to solve my emotional problems. But what really shook me up—and got me started on the path that changed my life—was Operation Desert Storm in early 1991. I sent three children off to the Persian Gulf War—my son-in-law Matt, a medic in Special Forces; my daughter Becky, a full-time college student and member of a medical unit in the Army Reserve; and my son James, a member of the Inactive Army Reserve reactivated as a chemicals expert.

Somehow, knowing that my children were putting their lives on the line got me thinking about my own mortality—and I knew in my heart the last thing they needed while they were overseas was to get a letter from home saying that their mother was ill because of a food-related problem.

The day I drove the third child to the airport to leave for Saudi Arabia, something happened to me that would change my life for the better—and forever. I stopped praying my constant prayer as a professional dieter, which was simply, "Please, God, let me lose ten pounds by Friday." Instead, I began praying, "God, please help me not be a burden to my kids and my family."

I quit praying for what I wanted, and started praying for what I needed—and in the process my prayers were answered. I couldn't keep the kids safe—that was out of my hands—but I could try to get healthier to better handle the stress of it. It was the least I could do on the homefront.

That quiet prayer was the beginning of the new JoAnna Lund. My initial goal was not to lose weight or create healthy recipes. I only wanted to become healthier for my kids, my husband, and myself.

Each of my children returned safely from the Persian Gulf War. But something didn't come back—the 130 extra pounds I'd been lugging around for far too long. I'd finally accepted the truth after all those agonizing years of suffering through on-again, off-again dieting.

There are no "magic" cures in life.

No "magic" potion, pill, or diet will make unwanted pounds disappear.

I found something better than magic, if you can believe it. When I turned my weight and health dilemma over to God for guidance, a new JoAnna Lund and Healthy Exchanges were born.

I discovered a new way to live my life—and uncovered an unexpected talent for creating easy "common folk" healthy recipes and sharing my commonsense approach to healthy living. I learned that I could motivate others to change their lives and adopt a positive outlook. I began publishing cookbooks and a monthly food newsletter, and speaking to groups all over the country.

I like to say, *"When life handed me a lemon, not only did I make healthy, tasty lemonade, I wrote the recipe down!"*

What I finally found was not a quick fix or a short-term diet, but a great way to live well for a lifetime.

I want to share it with you.

Healthy Exchanges®

Weight Loss

Choices™/Exchanges

If you've ever been on one of the national weight-loss programs like Weight Watchers or Diet Center, you've already been introduced to the concept of measured portions of different food groups that make up your daily food plan. If you are not familiar with such a system of weight-loss choices or exchanges, here's a brief explanation. (If you want or need more detailed information, you can write to the American Dietetic Association or the American Diabetes Association for comprehensive explanations.)

The idea of food exchanges is to divide foods into basic food groups. The foods in each group are measured in servings that have comparable values. These groups include Proteins/Meats, Breads/Starches, Vegetables, Fats, Fruits, Skim Milk, Free Foods, and Optional Calories.

Each choice or exchange included in a particular group has about the same number of calories and a similar carbohydrate, protein, and fat content as the other foods in that group. Because any food on a particular list can be "exchanged" for any other food in that group, it makes sense to call the food groups *exchanges* or *choices*.

I like to think we are also "exchanging" bad habits and food choices for good ones!

By using Weight Loss Choices™ or exchanges you can choose from a variety of foods without having to calculate the nutrient value of each one. This makes it easier to include a wide variety of foods in your daily menus and gives you the opportunity to tailor your choices to your unique appetite.

If you want to lose weight, you should consult your physician or other weight-control expert regarding the number of servings that would be best for you from each food group. Since men generally require more calories than women, and since the requirements for growing children and teenagers differ from those of adults, the right number of exchanges for any one person is a personal decision.

I have included a suggested plan of weight-loss choices in the pages following the exchange lists. It's a program I used to lose 130 pounds, and it's the one I still follow today.

(If you are a diabetic or have been diagnosed with heart problems, it is best to meet with your physician before using this or any other food program or recipe collection.)

Food Group Weight Loss Choices/Exchanges

Not all food group exchanges are alike. The ones that follow are for anyone who's interested in weight loss or maintenance. If you are a diabetic, you should check with your health-care provider or dietitian to get the information you need to help you plan your diet. Diabetic exchanges are calculated by the American Diabetic Association, and information about them is provided in *The Diabetic's Healthy Exchange Cookbook* (Perigee Books).

Every Healthy Exchanges recipe provides calculations in three ways:

• Weight Loss Choices/Exchanges

• Calories, Fat, Protein, Carbohydrates, and Fiber Grams, and Sodium in milligrams

• Diabetic Exchanges calculated for me by a Registered Dietitian

Healthy Exchanges recipes can help you eat well and recover your health, whatever your health concerns may be. Please take a few minutes to review the exchange lists and the suggestions that follow on how to count them. You have lots of great eating in store for you!

Proteins

Meat, poultry, seafood, eggs, cheese, and legumes.

One exchange of Protein is approximately 60 calories. Examples of one Protein choice or exchange:

1 ounce cooked weight of lean meat, poultry, or seafood
2 ounces white fish
1½ ounces 97% fat-free ham
1 egg (limit to no more than 4 per week)
¼ cup egg substitute
3 egg whites
¾ ounce reduced-fat cheese
½ cup fat-free cottage cheese
2 ounces cooked or ¾ ounces uncooked dry beans
1 tablespoon peanut butter (also count 1 fat exchange)

Breads

Breads, crackers, cereals, grains, and starchy vegetables. One exchange of Bread is approximately 80 calories. Examples of one Bread choice/exchange:

1 slice bread or 2 slices reduced-calorie bread (40 calories or less)
1 roll, any type (1 ounce)
½ cup cooked pasta or ¾ ounce uncooked (scant ½ cup)
½ cup cooked rice or 1 ounce uncooked (⅓ cup)
3 tablespoons flour
¾ ounce cold cereal
½ cup cooked hot cereal or ¾ ounce uncooked (2 tablespoons)
½ cup corn (kernels or cream style) or peas
4 ounces white potato, cooked, or 5 ounces uncooked
3 ounces sweet potato, cooked, or 4 ounces uncooked
3 cups air-popped popcorn
7 fat-free crackers (¾ ounce)
3 (2½-inch squares) graham crackers
2 (¾-ounce) rice cakes or 6 mini
1 tortilla, any type (6-inch diameter)

Fruits

All fruits and fruit juices. One exchange of Fruit is approximately 60 calories. Examples of one Fruit choice or exchange:

1 small apple or ½ cup slices
1 small orange
½ medium banana
¾ cup berries (except strawberries and cranberries)
1 cup strawberries or cranberries
½ cup canned fruit, packed in fruit juice or rinsed well
2 tablespoons raisins
1 tablespoon spreadable fruit spread
½ cup apple juice (4 fluid ounces)
½ cup orange juice (4 fluid ounces)
½ cup applesauce

Skim Milk

Milk, buttermilk, and yogurt. One exchange of Skim Milk is approximately 90 calories. Examples of one Skim Milk choice or exchange:

1 cup skim milk
½ cup evaporated skim milk
1 cup low-fat buttermilk
¾ cup plain fat-free yogurt
⅓ cup nonfat dry milk powder

Vegetables

All fresh, canned, or frozen vegetables other than the starchy vegetables. One exchange of Vegetables is approximately 30 calories. Examples of one Vegetable choice or exchange:

½ cup vegetable
¼ cup tomato sauce
1 medium fresh tomato
½ cup vegetable juice

Fats

Margarine, mayonnaise, vegetable oils, salad dressings, olives, and nuts. One exchange of fat is approximately 40 calories. Examples of one Fat choice or exchange:

> 1 teaspoon margarine or 2 teaspoons reduced-calorie margarine
> 1 teaspoon butter
> 1 teaspoon vegetable oil
> 1 teaspoon mayonnaise or 2 teaspoons reduced-calorie mayonnaise
> 1 teaspoon peanut butter
> 1 ounce olives
> ¼ ounce pecans or walnuts

Free Foods

Foods that do not provide nutritional value but are used to enhance the taste of foods are included in the Free Foods group. Examples of these are spices, herbs, extracts, vinegar, lemon juice, mustard, Worcestershire sauce, and soy sauce. Cooking sprays and artificial sweeteners used in moderation are also included in this group. However, you'll see that I include the caloric value of artificial sweeteners in the Optional Calories of the recipes.

You may occasionally see a recipe that lists "free food" as part of the portion. According to the published exchange lists, a free food contains fewer than 20 calories per serving. Two or three servings per day of free foods/drinks are usually allowed in a meal plan.

Optional Calories

Foods that do not fit into any other group but are used in moderation in recipes are included in Optional Calories. Foods that are counted in this way include sugar-free gelatin and puddings, fat-free mayonnaise and dressings, reduced-calorie whipped toppings, reduced-calorie syrups and jams, chocolate chips, coconut, and canned broth.

Sliders™

These are 80 Optional Calorie increments that do not fit into any particular category. You can choose which food groups to *slide* them into. It is wise to limit this selection to approximately three per day to ensure the best possible nutrition for your body while still enjoying an occasional treat.

Sliders may be used in either of the following ways:

1. If you have consumed all your Protein, Bread, Fruit, or Skim Milk Weight Loss Choices for the day, and you want to eat additional foods from those food groups, you simply use a Slider. It's what I call "healthy horse trading." Remember that Sliders may not be traded for choices in the Vegetables or Fats food groups.

2. Sliders may also be deducted from your Optional Calories (OC) for the day or week. ¼ Sl equals 20 OC; ½ Sl equals 40 OC; ¾ Sl equals 60 OC; and 1 Sl equals 80 OC. This way, you can choose the food group to *slide* into.

Healthy Exchanges
Weight Loss Choices

Here's my suggested program of Weight Loss Choices, based on an average daily total of 1,400–1,600 calories per day. *If you require more or fewer calories, please revise this plan to your individual needs.*

Each day, women should plan to eat:

2 Skim Milk servings, 90 calories each
2 Fat servings, 40 calories each
3 Fruit servings, 60 calories each
4 Vegetable servings or more, 30 calories each
5 Protein servings, 60 calories each
5 Bread servings, 80 calories each

Men should add to this basic program: 2 Fat servings (for a total of 4), 1 Protein serving (for a total of 6), and 2 Bread servings (for a total of 7).

Young people should follow the program for Men but add 1 Skim Milk serving for a total of 3 servings.

You may also choose to add up to 100 Optional Calories per day, and up to 28 Sliders per week at 80 calories each. If you choose to include more Sliders in your daily or weekly totals, deduct those 80 calories from your Optional Calorie "bank."

A word about **Sliders**. These are to be counted toward your totals after you have used your allotment of choices of Skim Milk, Protein, Bread, and Fruit for the day. By "sliding" an additional choice into one of these groups, you can meet your individual needs for that day. Sliders are especially helpful when traveling, stressed out, eating out, or for special events. I often use mine so I can enjoy my favorite Healthy Exchanges desserts. Vegetables are not to be counted as Sliders. Enjoy as many Vegetable choices as you need to ·feel satisfied. Because we want to limit our fat intake to moderate amounts, additional Fat choices should not be counted as Sliders. If you choose to include more fat on an *occasional* basis, count the extra choices as Optional Calories.

Keep a daily food diary of your Weight Loss Choices, checking off what you eat as you go. If, at the end of the day, your required selections are not 100 percent accounted for, but you have done the best you could, go to bed with a clear conscience. There will be days when you have ¼ Fruit or ½ Bread left over. What are you going to do—eat two slices of an orange or half a slice of bread and throw the rest out? I always say that "nothing in life comes out exact." Just do the best you can . . . *the best you can.*

Try to drink at least eight glasses of water a day. Water truly is the "nectar" of good health.

As a little added insurance, I take a multivitamin each day. It's not essential, but if my day's worth of well-planned meals "bites the dust" when unexpected events intrude on my regular routine, my body still gets its vital nutrients.

The calories listed in each group of choices are averages. Some choices within each group may be higher or lower, so it's important to select a variety of different foods instead of eating the same three or four all the time.

Use your Optional Calories! They are what I call "life's little extras." They make all the difference in how you enjoy your food and appreciate the variety available to you. Yes, we can get by without them, but do you really want to? Keep in mind that you should be using all your daily Weight Loss Choices first to ensure you are getting the basics of good nutrition. But I guarantee that Optional Calories will keep you from feeling deprived—and help you reach your weight-loss goals.

Sodium, Fat, Cholesterol, and Processed Foods

*A*re Healthy Exchanges Ingredients Really Healthy?
When I first created Healthy Exchanges, many people asked about sodium, about whether it was necessary to calculate the percentage of fat, saturated fat, and cholesterol in a healthy diet, and about my use of processed foods in many recipes. I researched these questions as I was developing my program, so you can feel confident about using the recipes and food plan.

Sodium

Most people consume more sodium than their bodies need. The American Heart Association and the American Diabetes Association recommend limiting daily sodium intake to no more than 3,000 mg. per day. If your doctor suggests you limit your sodium even more, then *you really must read labels.*

Sodium is an essential nutrient and should not be completely eliminated. It helps to regulate blood volume and is needed for normal daily muscle and nerve functions. Most of us, however, have no trouble getting "all we need" and then some.

As with everything else, moderation is my approach. I rarely ever have salt in my list as an added ingredient. But if you're especially sodium sensitive, make the right choices for you—and save high-sodium foods such as sauerkraut for an occasional treat.

I use lots of spices to enhance flavors, so you won't notice the absence of salt. In the few cases where it is used, it's vital for the success of the recipe, so please don't omit it.

When I do use an ingredient high in sodium, I try to compensate by using low-sodium products in the remainder of the recipe. Many fat-free products are a little higher in sodium to make up for any flavor that disappeared along with the fat. But when I take advantage of these fat-free, higher-sodium products, I stretch that ingredient within the recipe, lowering the amount of sodium per serving. A good example is my use of fat-free canned soups. While the suggested number of servings per can is two, I make sure my final creation serves at least four and sometimes six. So the soup's sodium has been "watered down" from one-third to one-half of the original amount.

Even if you don't have to watch your sodium intake for medical reasons, using moderation is another "healthy exchange" to make on your own journey to good health.

Fat Percentages

We've been told that 30 percent is the magic number—that we should limit fat intake to 30 percent or less of our total calories. It's good advice, and I try to have a weekly average of 15 to 25 percent myself. I believe any less than 15 percent is really just another restrictive diet that won't last. And more than 25 percent on a regular basis is too much of a good thing.

When I started listing fat grams along with calories in my recipes, I was tempted to include the percentage of calories from fat. After all, in the vast majority of my recipes, that percentage is well below 30 percent. This even includes my pie recipes that allow you a realistic serving instead of many "diet" recipes that tell you a serving is 1/12 of a pie.

Figuring fat grams is easy enough. Each gram of fat equals nine calories. Multiply fat grams by 9 then divide that number by the total calories to get the percentage of calories from fat.

So why don't I do it? After consulting four registered dietitians for advice, I decided to omit this information. They felt that it's too easy for people to become obsessed by that 30 percent figure, which is after all supposed to be a percentage of total calories over the course of a day or a week. We mustn't feel we can't include a healthy ingredient such as pecans or olives in one recipe just because, on its own, it has more than 30 percent of its calories from fat.

An example of this would be a casserole made with 90 percent lean red meat. Most of us benefit from eating red meat in moderation, as it provides iron and niacin in our diets, and it also makes life more enjoyable for us and those who eat with us. If we *only* look at the percentage of calories from fat in a serving of this one dish, which might be as high as 40 to 45 percent, we might choose not to include this recipe in our weekly food plan.

The dietitians suggested that it's important to consider the total picture when making such decisions. As long as your overall food plan keeps fat calories to 30 percent, it's all right to enjoy an occasional dish that is somewhat higher in fat content. Healthy foods I include in **MODERATION** include 90 percent lean red meat, olives, and nuts. I don't eat these foods every day, and you may not either. But occasionally, in a good recipe, they make all the difference in the world between just getting by (deprivation) and truly enjoying your food.

Remember, the goal is eating in a healthy way so you can enjoy and live well the rest of your life.

Saturated Fats and Cholesterol

You'll see that I don't provide calculations for saturated fats or cholesterol amounts in my recipes. It's for the simple and yet not so simple reason that accurate, up-to-date, brand-specific information can be difficult to obtain from food manufacturers, especially since the way in which they produce food keeps changing rapidly. But once more I've consulted with registered dietitians and other professionals and found that because I use only a few products that are high in saturated fat, and use them in such limited quantities, my recipes are suitable for patients concerned about controlling or lowering cholesterol. You'll also find that whenever I do use one of these ingredients *in moderation*, everything else in the recipe, and in the meals my family and I enjoy, is low in fat.

Processed Foods

Some people have asked how "healthy" recipes can so often use "processed foods"—ready-made products like canned soups, prepared piecrusts, frozen potatoes, and frozen whipped topping? Well, I believe that such foods, used properly (that word **moderation** again) as part of a healthy lifestyle, have a place as ingredients in healthy recipes.

I'm not in favor of spraying everything we eat with chemicals, and I don't mean that all our foods should come out of packages. But I do think we should use the best available products to make cooking easier and foods taste better. I take advantage of good low-fat and low-sugar products, and my recipes are created for busy people like me who want to eat well and eat healthy. I don't expect people to visit out-of-the-way health food stores or find time to cook beans from scratch—*because I don't*. There are lots of very good processed foods available in your local grocery store, and they can make it so much easier to enjoy the benefits of healthy eating.

I certainly don't recommend that everything you eat come from a can, box, or jar. In the best of all possible worlds I would start with the basics: rice, poultry, fish, or beef, and raw vegetables—then throw in a can of reduced-sodium/97 percent fat-free soup (a processed food), and end up with an appetizing, easy-to-prepare, healthy meal.

Most of us can't grow fresh food in the backyard, and many people don't even have a nearby farmer's market. But instead of saying, "Well, I can't get to the health food store so why not eat that hot fudge sundae?" you gotta play ball in your private ball field, not in someone else's. I want to help you figure out ways to make living healthy **doable** and **livable** *wherever you live*, or you're not going to stick with it.

I've checked with the American Dietetic Association, the American Diabetes Association, and with many registered dietitians, and

I've been assured that sugar-free and fat-free processed products that use substitutes for sugar and fat are safe when used in the intended way. This means a realistic serving, not one hundred cans of diet soda every day of the year! Even carrots can turn your skin orange if you eat far too many, but does anyone suggest we avoid eating carrots?

Of course, it is your privilege to disagree with me and to use whatever you choose when you prepare your food. I never want to be one of those "opinionated" people who think it's their God-given right to make personal decisions for others and insist that their way is the *only* way.

Besides, new research comes out every day that declares one food bad and another food good. Then a few days later, some new information emerges, saying that the opposite is true. When the facts are sifted from the fiction, the truth is probably somewhere in between. I know I feel confused when what was bad for you last year is good for you now, and vice versa.

Instead of listening to unreasonable sermons by naysayers who are nowhere around when it comes time to make a quick and healthy meal for your family, I've tried to incorporate the best processed foods I can find into my Healthy Exchanges recipes. I get stacks of mail from people who are thrilled to discover they can eat good-tasting food and who proudly use processed foods in the intended way. I think you will agree that my commonsense approach to healthy cooking is the right choice for many. Because these foods are convenient, tasty, and good substitutes for less healthy products, people are willing to use them long-term.

So don't let anyone make you feel ashamed for including these products in your healthy lifestyle. Only you can decide what's best for you and your family's needs. Part of living a healthy lifestyle is making those decisions and *getting on with life*.

JoAnna's Ten Commandments of Successful Cooking

A few minutes spent before you start cooking will save you hours in the kitchen. The best use of your time, energy, and money is not only reading these suggestions for conquering the kitchen but also applying them to your daily cooking.

1. **Read the entire recipe from start to finish** and be sure you understand the process involved. Check that you have all the equipment you will need *before* you begin.

2. **Check the ingredient list** and be sure you have *everything* and in the amounts required. Keep cooking sprays handy—while they're not listed as ingredients, I use them all the time (just a quick squirt!).

3. **Set out *all* the ingredients and equipment needed** to prepare the recipe on the counter near you *before* you start. Remember that old saying, *A stitch in time saves nine.* It applies in the kitchen, too.

4. **Do as much advance preparation as possible** before actually cooking. Chop, cut, grate, or do whatever is needed to prepare the ingredients and have them ready before you start to mix. Turn the oven on at least ten minutes before putting food in to bake, to allow the oven to preheat to the proper temperature.

5. **Use a kitchen timer** to tell you when the cooking or baking time is up. Because stove temperatures vary slightly by manufacturer, you may want to set your timer for five minutes less than the suggested time just to prevent overcooking. Check the progress of your dish at that time, then decide if you need the additional minutes or not.

6. **Measure carefully**. Use glass measures for liquids and metal or plastic cups for dry ingredients. My recipes are based on standard measurements. Unless I tell you it's a scant or full cup, measure the cup level.

7. **For best results, follow the recipe instructions exactly**. Feel free to substitute ingredients that *don't tamper* with the basic chemistry of the recipe, but be sure to leave key ingredients alone. For example, you could substitute sugar-free instant chocolate pudding for sugar-free instant butterscotch pudding, but if you used a six-serving package when a four-serving package was listed in the ingredients, or you used instant when cook-and-serve is required, you won't get the right result.

8. **Clean up as you go**. It is much easier to wash a few items at a time than to face a whole counter of dirty dishes later. The same is true for spills on the counter or floor.

9. **Be careful about doubling or halving a recipe**. Though many recipes can be altered successfully to serve more or fewer people, *many cannot*. This is especially true when it comes to spices and liquids. If you try to double a recipe that calls for one teaspoon of pumpkin-pie spice, for example, and you double the spice, you may end up with a too-spicy taste. I usually suggest increasing spices or liquid by 1½ times when doubling a recipe. If it tastes a little bland to you, you can increase the spice to 1¾ times the original amount the next time you prepare the dish. Remember you can always add more, but you can't take it out after it's been stirred in.

The same is true with liquid ingredients. If you wanted to triple a recipe like my Macho Burritos because you were planning to serve a crowd, you might think you should use three times as much of every ingredient. Don't, or you could end up with Burrito Soup! The original recipe calls for 1¾ cups of chunky tomato sauce, so I'd suggest using 3½ cups of sauce when you triple the recipe (or 2¾ cups if you double it). You'll still have a good-tasting dish that won't run all over the plate.

10. **Write your reactions next to each recipe once you've served it**. Yes, that's right, I'm giving you permission to write in this book. It's yours, after all. Ask yourself: Did everyone like it? Did I have to add another half teaspoon of chili seasoning to please my family, who like to live on the spicier side of the street? You may even want to rate the recipe on a scale of 1★ to 4★, depending on what you thought of it. (Four stars would be the top rating—and I hope you'll feel that way about many of my recipes.) Jotting down your comments while they are fresh in your mind will help you personalize the recipe to your own taste the next time you prepare it.

My Best Healthy Exchanges Tips and Tidbits

Measurements, General Cooking Tips, and Basic Ingredients

The word **moderation** best describes **my use of fats, sugar substitutes, and sodium** in these recipes. Wherever possible, I've used cooking spray for sautéing and for browning meats and vegetables. I also use reduced-calorie margarine and no-fat mayonnaise and salad dressings. Lean ground turkey *or* ground beef can be used in the recipes. Just be sure whatever you choose is at least *90 percent lean.*

I've also included **small amounts of sugar and brown sugar substitutes as the sweetening agent** in many of the recipes. I don't drink a hundred cans of soda a day or eat enough artificially sweetened foods in a twenty-four-hour time period to be troubled by sugar substitutes. But if this is a concern of yours and you *do not* need to watch your sugar intake, you can always replace the sugar substitutes with processed sugar and the sugar-free products with regular ones.

I created my recipes knowing they would also be used by hypoglycemics, diabetics, and those concerned about triglycerides. If you choose to use sugar instead, be sure to count the additional calories.

A word of caution when cooking with *sugar substitutes*: Use *saccharin*-based sweeteners when *heating or baking.* In recipes that don't require heat, **Aspartame** (known as NutraSweet) works well in uncooked dishes but leaves an aftertaste in baked products.

I'm often asked why I use an **8-by-8-inch baking dish** in my recipes. It's for portion control. If the recipe says it serves four, just cut down the center, turn the dish, and cut again. Like magic, there's your serving. Also, if this is the only recipe you are preparing requiring an oven, the square dish fits into a tabletop toaster oven easily and energy can be conserved.

To make life even easier, **whenever a recipe calls for ounce measurements** (other than raw meats) I've included the closest cup equivalent. I need to use my scale daily when creating recipes, so I've measured for you at the same time.

Most of the recipes are for **4 to 6 servings.** If you don't have that many to feed, do what I do: freeze individual portions. Then all you have to do is choose something from the freezer and take it to work for lunch or have your evening meals prepared in advance for the week. In this way, I always have something on hand that is both good to eat and good for me.

Unless a recipe includes hard-boiled eggs, cream cheese, mayonnaise, or a raw vegetable or fruit, **the leftovers should freeze well.** (I've marked recipes that freeze well with the symbol of a **snowflake ❋.**) This includes most of the cream pies. Divide any recipe up into individual servings and freeze for your own "TV" dinners.

Another good idea is **cutting leftover pie into individual pieces and freezing each one separately** in a small Ziploc freezer bag. Then the next time you want to thaw a piece of pie for yourself, you don't have to thaw the whole pie. It's great this way for brown-bag lunches, too. Just pull a piece out of the freezer on your way to work and by lunchtime you will have a wonderful dessert waiting for you.

Unless I specify **"covered" for simmering or baking,** prepare my recipes **uncovered.** Occasionally you will read a recipe that asks you to cover a dish for a time, then to uncover, so read the directions carefully to avoid confusion—and to get the best results.

Low-fat cooking spray is another blessing in a Healthy Exchanges kitchen. It's currently available in three flavors . . .

- OLIVE OIL–FLAVORED when cooking Mexican, Italian, or Greek dishes

- BUTTER FLAVORED when the hint of butter is desired

- REGULAR for everything else

A quick spray of the butter-flavored kind makes air-popped popcorn a low-fat taste treat, or try it as a butter substitute on steaming hot corn on the cob. One light spray of the skillet when browning meat will convince you that you're using "old fashioned fat," and a quick coating of the casserole dish before you add the ingredients will make serving easier and cleanup quicker.

I use reduced-sodium **canned chicken broth** in place of dry bouillon to lower the sodium content. The intended flavor is still present in the prepared dish. As a reduced-sodium beef broth is not currently available (at least not in DeWitt, Iowa), I use the canned regular beef broth. The sodium content is still lower than regular dry bouillon.

Whenever **cooked rice or pasta** is an ingredient, follow the package directions, but eliminate the salt and/or margarine called for. This helps lower the sodium and fat content. It tastes just fine; trust me on this.

Here's another tip: When **cooking rice or noodles**, why not cook extra "for the pot"? After you use what you need, store leftover rice in a covered container (where it will keep for a couple of days). With noodles like spaghetti or macaroni, first rinse and drain as usual, then measure out what you need. Put the leftovers, covered with water, in a bowl, then store in the refrigerator, covered, until they're needed. Then, measure out what you need, rinse and drain them, and they're ready to go.

Does your **pita bread** often tear before you can make a sandwich? Here's my tip to make it open easily: cut the bread in half, put the halves in the microwave for about 15 seconds, and they will open up by themselves. Voilà!

When **chunky salsa** is listed as an ingredient, I leave the degree of "heat" up to your personal taste. In our house, I'm considered a wimp. I go for the "mild" while Cliff prefers "extra-hot." How do we compromise? I prepare the recipe with mild salsa because he can always add a spoonful or two of the hotter version to his serving, but I can't enjoy the dish if it's too spicy for me.

Proteins

I use eggs in moderation. I enjoy the real thing on an average of three to four times a week. So, my recipes are calculated on using whole eggs. However, if you choose to use egg substitutes in place of the egg, the finished product will turn out just fine and the fat grams per serving will be even lower than those listed.

If you like the look, taste, and feel of **hard-boiled eggs** in salads but haven't been using them because of the cholesterol in the yolk, I have a couple of alternatives for you. (1) Pour an 8-ounce carton of egg substitute into a medium skillet sprayed with cooking spray. Cover skillet tightly and cook over low heat until substitute is just set, about 10 minutes. Remove from heat and let set, still covered, for 10 minutes more. Uncover and cool completely. Chop set mixture. This will make about 1 cup of chopped egg. (2) Even easier is to hard-boil "real eggs," toss the yolk away, and chop the white. Either way, you don't deprive yourself of the pleasure of egg in your salad.

In most recipes calling for **egg substitutes**, you can use 2 egg whites in place of the equivalent of 1 egg substitute. Just break the eggs open and toss the yolks away. I can hear some of you already saying, "But that's wasteful!" Well, take a look at the price on the egg substitute package (which usually has the equivalent of 4 eggs in it), then look at the price of a dozen eggs, from which you'd get the equivalent of 6 egg substitutes. Now, what's wasteful about that?

Whenever I include **cooked chicken** in a recipe, I use roasted white meat without skin. Whenever I include **roast beef or pork** in a recipe, I use the loin cuts because they are much leaner. However, most of the time, I do my roasting of all these meats at the local deli. I just ask for a chunk of their lean roasted meat, 6 or 8 ounces, and ask them to slice it. When I get home, I cube or dice the meat and am ready to use it in my recipe. The reason I do this is threefold. (1) I'm getting just the amount I need without leftovers. (2) I don't have the expense of heating the oven. (3) I'm not throwing away the bone, gristle, and fat I'd be cutting away from the meat. Overall, it is probably cheaper to "roast" it the way I do.

Did you know that you can make an acceptable meat loaf without using egg for the binding? Just replace every egg with ¼ cup of liquid. You could use beef broth, tomato sauce, even applesauce, to name just a few alternatives. For a meat loaf to serve six, I always use one pound of extra-lean ground beef or turkey, six tablespoons of dried fine bread crumbs, and ¼ cup of the liquid, plus anything else healthy that strikes my fancy at the time. I mix well and place the mixture in an 8-by-8-inch baking dish or 9-by-5-inch loaf pan sprayed with cooking spray. Bake uncovered at 350 degrees for 35 to 50 minutes (depending on the added ingredients). You will never miss the egg.

Anytime you are **browning ground meat** for a casserole and want to get rid of almost all of the excess fat, just place the uncooked meat loosely in a plastic colander. Set the colander in a glass pie plate. Place in a microwave and cook on High for three to six minutes (depending on the amount being browned), stirring often. Use as you would for any casserole. You can also chop up onions and brown them with the meat if you want to.

Milk and Yogurt

Take it from me—nonfat dry milk powder is great! I *do not* use it for drinking, but I *do* use it for cooking. Three good reasons why:

1. It is very **inexpensive**.

2. It **does not sour** because you use it only as needed. Store the box in your refrigerator or freezer and it will keep almost forever.

3. You can easily **add extra calcium** to just about any recipe without added liquid.

I consider nonfat dry milk powder one of Mother Nature's modern-day miracles of convenience. But do purchase a good national name brand (I like Carnation), and keep it fresh by proper storage.

In many of my pies and puddings, I use nonfat dry milk powder and water instead of skim milk. Usually I call for ⅔ cup nonfat dry milk powder and 1¼ to 1½ cups water or liquid. This way I can get the nutrients of two cups of milk, but much less liquid, and the end result is much creamier. Also, the recipe sets up more quickly, usually in 5 minutes or less. So if someone knocks at your door unexpectedly at mealtime, you can quickly throw a pie together and enjoy it minutes later.

You can make your own "**sour cream**" by combining ¾ cup plain fat-free yogurt with ⅓ cup nonfat dry milk powder. What you did by doing this is fourfold: (1) The dry milk stabilizes the yogurt and keeps the whey from separating. (2) The dry milk slightly helps to cut the tartness of the yogurt. (3) It's still virtually fat-free. (4) The calcium has been increased by 100 percent. Isn't it great how we can make that distant relative of sour cream a first kissin' cousin by adding the nonfat dry milk powder? Or, if you place 1 cup of plain fat-free yogurt in a sieve lined with a coffee filter, and place the sieve over a small bowl and refrigerate for about 6 hours, you will end up with a very good alternative for sour cream. To **stabilize yogurt** when cooking or baking with it, just add 1 teaspoon cornstarch to every ¾ cup yogurt.

If a recipe calls for **evaporated skim milk** and you don't have any in the cupboard, make your own. For every ½ cup evaporated skim milk needed, combine ⅓ cup nonfat dry milk powder and ½ cup water. Use as you would evaporated skim milk.

You can also make your own **sugar-free and fat-free sweetened condensed milk** at home. Combine 1⅓ cups nonfat dry milk powder and ½ cup cold water in a 2-cup glass measure. Cover and microwave on High until mixture is hot but *not* boiling. Stir in ½ cup Sprinkle Sweet or Sugar Twin. Cover and refrigerate at least 4 hours. This mixture will keep for up to two weeks in the refrigerator. Use in just about any recipe that calls for sweetened condensed milk.

For any recipe that calls for **buttermilk**, you might want to try Jo's Buttermilk: Blend one cup of water and ⅔ cup dry milk powder (the nutrients of two cups of skim milk). It'll be thicker than this mixed-up milk usually is, because it's doubled. Add 1 teaspoon white vinegar and stir, then let it sit for at least ten minutes.

One of my subscribers was looking for a way to further restrict salt intake and needed a substitute for **cream of mushroom soup**. For many of my recipes, I use Healthy Request Cream of Mushroom soup, as it is a reduced-sodium product. The label suggests two servings per can, but I usually incorporate the soup into a recipe serving at least four. By doing this, I've reduced the sodium in the soup by half again.

But if you must restrict your sodium even more, try making my Healthy Exchanges **Creamy Mushroom Sauce**. Place 1½ cups evaporated skim milk and 3 tablespoons flour in a covered jar. Shake well and pour mixture into a medium saucepan sprayed with butter-flavored cooking spray. Add ½ cup canned sliced mushrooms, rinsed and drained. Cook over medium heat, stirring often, until mixture thickens. Add any seasonings of your choice. You can use this sauce in any recipe that calls for one 10¾-ounce can of cream of mushroom soup.

Why did I choose these proportions and ingredients?

- 1½ cups of evaporated skim milk is the amount in one can.

- It's equal to three milk choices or exchanges.

- It's the perfect amount of liquid and flour for a medium cream sauce.

- Three tablespoons of flour are equal to one Bread/Starch choice or exchange.

- Any leftovers will reheat beautifully with a flour-based sauce, but not with a cornstarch base.

- The mushrooms are one vegetable choice or exchange.

- This sauce is virtually fat free, sugar free, and sodium free.

Fruits and Vegetables

If you want to enjoy a **"fruit shake"** with some pizazz, just combine soda water and unsweetened fruit juice in a blender. Add crushed ice. Blend on High until thick. Refreshment without guilt.

You'll see that many recipes use ordinary **canned vegetables**. They're much cheaper than reduced-sodium versions, and once you rinse and drain them, the sodium is reduced anyway. I believe in saving money wherever possible so we can afford the best in fat-free and sugar-free products as they come onto the market.

All three kinds of **vegetables—fresh, frozen, and canned—** have their place in a healthy diet. My husband, Cliff, hates the taste of frozen or fresh green beans, thinks the texture is all wrong, so I use canned green beans instead. In this case, canned vegetables have their proper place when I'm feeding my husband. If someone in your family has a similar concern, it's important to respond to it so everyone can be happy and enjoy the meal.

When I use **fruits or vegetables** like apples, cucumbers, and zucchini, I wash them really well and **leave their skin on**. It provides added color, fiber, and attractiveness to any dish. And, because I use processed flour in my cooking, I like to increase the fiber in my diet by eating my fruits and vegetables in their closest-to-natural state.

To help keep **fresh fruits and veggies fresh**, just give them a quick "shower" with lemon juice. The easiest way to do this is to pour purchased lemon juice into a kitchen spray bottle and store in the refrigerator. Then, every time you use fresh fruits or vegetables in a salad or dessert, simply give them a quick spray with your "lemon spritzer." You just might be amazed by how well this little trick keeps your produce from turning brown so fast.

The next time you warm canned vegetables such as carrots or green beans, drain and heat the vegetables in ¼ cup beef or chicken broth. It gives a nice variation to an old standby. Here's how a simple **white sauce** for vegetables and casseroles can be made without using added fat by spraying a medium saucepan with butter-flavored cooking spray: Place 1½ cups evaporated skim milk and 3 tablespoons flour in a covered jar. Shake well. Pour into sprayed saucepan and cook over medium heat until thick, stirring constantly. Add salt and pepper to taste. You can also add ½ cup canned drained mushrooms and/or 3 ounces (¾ cup) shredded reduced-fat cheese. Continue cooking until cheese melts.

Zip up canned or frozen green beans with **chunky salsa**: ½ cup to 2 cups beans. Heat thoroughly. Chunky salsa also makes a wonderful dressing on lettuce salads. It only counts as a vegetable, so enjoy.

Another wonderful **South of the Border** dressing can be stirred up by using ½ cup of chunky salsa and ¼ cup of fat-free Ranch dressing. Cover and store in your refrigerator. Use as a dressing for salads or as a topping for baked potatoes.

For **gravy** with all the "old time" flavor but without the extra fat, try this almost effortless way to prepare it. (It's almost as easy as opening up a store-bought jar.) Pour the juice off your roasted meat, then set the roast aside to "rest" for about 20 minutes. Place the juice in an uncovered cake pan or other large flat pan (we want the large air surface to speed up the cooling process) and put it in the freezer until the fat congeals on top and you can skim it off. Or, if you prefer, use a skimming pitcher purchased at your kitchen gadget store. Either way, measure about 1½ cups skimmed broth and pour into a medium saucepan. Cook over medium heat until heated through, about five minutes. In a covered jar, combine ½ cup water or cooled potato broth with 3 tablespoons flour. Shake well. Pour flour mixture into warmed juice. Combine well using a wire whisk. Continue cooking until gravy thickens, about 5 minutes. Season with salt and pepper to taste.

Why did I use flour instead of cornstarch? Because any leftovers will reheat nicely with the flour base and would not with a cornstarch base. Also, 3 tablespoons of flour works out to 1 Bread/Starch exchange. This virtually fat-free gravy makes about 2 cups, so you could spoon about ½ cup gravy on your low-fat mashed potatoes and only have to count your gravy as ¼ Bread/Starch exchange.

Desserts

Thaw **lite whipped topping** in the refrigerator overnight. Never try to force the thawing by stirring or using a microwave to soften. Stirring it will remove the air from the topping that gives it the lightness and texture we want, and there's not enough fat in it to survive being heated.

How can I **frost an entire pie with just ½ cup of whipped**

topping? First, don't use an inexpensive brand. I use Cool Whip Lite or La Creme lite. Make sure the topping is fully thawed. Always spread from the center to the sides using a rubber spatula. This way, ½ cup topping will literally cover an entire pie. Remember, the operative word is **frost**, not pile the entire container on top of the pie!

Here's a way to **extend the flavor (and oils) of purchased whipped topping:** Blend together ¾ cup plain nonfat yogurt and ⅓ cup nonfat dry milk powder. Add sugar substitute to equal 2 tablespoons sugar, 1 cup Cool Whip Lite and 1 teaspoon of the flavoring of your choice (vanilla, coconut, or almond are all good choices). Gently mix and use as you would whipped topping. The texture is almost a cross between marshmallow cream and whipped cream. This is enough to mound high on a pie.

For a different taste when preparing sugar-free instant pudding mixes, use ¾ cup plain fat-free yogurt for one of the required cups of milk. Blend as usual. It will be *thicker and creamier*. And, no it doesn't taste like yogurt. Another variation for the sugar-free instant vanilla pudding is to use 1 cup skim milk and 1 cup crushed pineapple juice. Mix as usual.

For a special treat that tastes anything but "diet," try placing **spreadable fruit** in a container and microwave for about 15 seconds. Then pour the melted fruit spread over a serving of nonfat ice cream or frozen yogurt. One tablespoon of spreadable fruit is equal to 1 fruit serving. Some combinations to get you started are apricot over chocolate ice cream, strawberry over strawberry ice cream, or any flavor over vanilla. Another way I use spreadable fruit is to make a delicious **topping for a cheesecake or angel food cake**. I take ½ cup of fruit and ½ cup Cool Whip Lite and blend the two together with a teaspoon of coconut extract.

Here's a really **good topping** for the fall of the year. Place 1½ cups of unsweetened applesauce in a medium saucepan or 4-cup glass measure. Stir in two tablespoons of raisins, 1 teaspoon of apple-pie spice, and two tablespoons of Cary's sugar-free maple syrup. Cook over medium heat on the stove or process on High in the microwave until warm. Then spoon about ½ cup of the warm mixture over pancakes, French toast, or fat-free and sugar-free vanilla ice cream. It's as close as you will get to guilt-free apple pie!

A quick yet tasty way to prepare **strawberries for shortcake** is to place about ¾ cup of sliced strawberries, 2 tablespoons of Diet Mountain Dew, and sugar substitute to equal ¼ cup sugar in a blender container. Process on Blend until the mixture is smooth. Pour the mixture into a bowl. Add 1¼ cups of sliced strawberries and mix well. Cover and refrigerate until ready to serve with short-cakes.

The next time you are making treats for the family, try using **unsweetened applesauce** for some or all of the required oil in the recipe. For instance, if the recipe calls for ½ cup of cooking oil, use up to the ½ cup in applesauce. It works and most people will not even notice the difference. It's great in purchased cake mixes, but so far I haven't been able to figure out a way to deep-fat fry with it!

Another trick I often use is to include tiny amounts of "real people" food, such as coconut, but extend the flavor by using extracts. Try it—you will be surprised by how little of the real thing you can use and still feel you are not being deprived.

If you are preparing a pie filling that has ample moisture, just line **graham crackers** in the bottom of a 9-by-9-inch cake pan. Pour the filling over the top of the crackers. Cover and refrigerate until the moisture has had enough time to soften the crackers. Overnight is best. This eliminates the added **fats and sugars of a piecrust**.

When **stirring fat-free cream cheese to soften it**, use only a sturdy spoon, never an electric mixer. The speed of a mixer can cause the cream cheese to lose its texture and become watery.

Did you know you can make your own **fruit-flavored yogurt?** Mix 1 tablespoon of any flavor of spreadable fruit spread with ¾ cup of plain yogurt. It's every bit as tasty and much cheaper. You can also make your own **lemon yogurt** by combining 3 cups of plain fat-free yogurt with 1 tub of Crystal Light lemonade powder. Mix well, cover, and store in the refrigerator. I think you will be pleasantly surprised by the ease, cost, and flavor of this "made from scratch" calcium-rich treat. P.S.: You can make any flavor you like by using any of the Crystal Light mixes—Cranberry? Iced tea? You decide.

Sugar-free puddings and gelatins are important to many of my recipes, but if you prefer to avoid sugar substitutes, you could still prepare the recipes with regular puddings or gelatins. The calories would be higher, but you would still be cooking low-fat.

When a recipe calls for **chopped nuts** (and you only have

whole ones), who wants to dirty the food processor just for a couple of tablespoons? You could try to chop them using your cutting board, but be prepared for bits and pieces to fly all over the kitchen. I use "Grandma's food processor." I take the biggest nuts I can find, put them in a small glass bowl, and chop them into chunks just the right size using a metal biscuit cutter.

If you have a **leftover muffin** and are looking for something a little different for breakfast, you can make a "**breakfast sundae.**" Crumble the muffin into a cereal bowl. Sprinkle a serving of fresh fruit over it and top with a couple of tablespoons of nonfat plain yogurt sweetened with sugar substitute and your choice of extract. The thought of it just might make you jump out of bed with a smile on your face. (Speaking of muffins, did you know that if you fill the unused muffin wells with water when baking muffins, you help ensure more even baking and protect the muffin pan at the same time?) Another muffin hint: lightly spray the inside of paper baking cups with butter-flavored cooking spray before spooning the muffin batter into them. Then you won't end up with paper clinging to your fresh-baked muffins.

The secret of making **good meringues** without sugar is to use 1 tablespoon of Sprinkle Sweet or Sugar Twin for every egg white, and a small amount of extract. Use ½ to 1 teaspoon for the batch. Almond, vanilla, and coconut are all good choices. Use the same amount of cream of tartar you usually do. Bake the meringue in the same old way. Don't think you can't have meringue pies because you can't eat sugar. You can, if you do it my way. (Remember that egg whites whip up best at room temperature.)

Homemade or Store-Bought?

I've been asked which is better for you, homemade from scratch or purchased foods. My answer is *both*! They each have a place in a healthy lifestyle, and what that place is has everything to do with you.

Take **piecrusts**, for instance. If you love spending your spare time in the kitchen preparing foods, and you're using low-fat, low-sugar, and reasonably low-sodium ingredients, go for it! But if, like so many people, your time is limited and you've learned to read labels, you could be better off using purchased foods.

I know that when I prepare a pie (and I experiment with a couple of pies each week, because this is Cliff's favorite dessert), I use a purchased crust. Why? Mainly because I can't make a good-tasting piecrust that is lower in fat than the brands I use. Also, purchased piecrusts fit my rule of "If it takes longer to cook it than eat it, forget it!"

I've checked the nutrient information for the purchased piecrust against recipes for traditional and "diet" piecrusts, using my computer software program. The purchased crust calculated lower in both fat and calories! I have tried some low-fat and low-sugar recipes, but they just don't spark my taste buds, or were so complicated you needed an engineering degree just to get the crust in the pie plate.

I'm very happy with the purchased piecrusts in my recipes, because the finished product rarely, if ever, has more than 30 percent of total calories coming from fat. I also believe that we have to prepare foods our families and friends will eat with us on a regular basis and not feel deprived, or we've wasted our time, energy, and money.

I could use a purchased "lite" **pie filling**, but instead I make my own. Here I can save both fat and sugar, and still make the filling almost as fast as opening a can. The bottom line: know what you have to spend when it comes to both time and fat/sugar calories, then make the best decision you can for you and your family. And don't go without an occasional piece of pie because you think it isn't *necessary*. A delicious pie prepared in a healthy way is one of the simple pleasures of life. It's a little thing, but it can make all the difference between just getting by with the bare minimum and living a full and healthy lifestyle.

Many people have experimented with my tip about **substituting applesauce and artificial sweetener for butter and sugar**, but what if you aren't satisfied with the result? One woman wrote to me about a recipe for her grandmother's cookies that called for 1 cup of butter and 1½ cups of sugar. Well, any recipe that depends on as much butter and sugar as this one does is generally not a good candidate for "healthy exchanges." The original recipe needed a large quantity of fat to produce the crisp cookies just like the ones Grandma made.

Unsweetened applesauce can be used to substitute for vegetable oil with various degrees of success, but not to replace butter, lard, or margarine. If your recipe calls for ½ cup oil or less, and it's a quick bread, muffin, or bar cookie, replacing the oil with applesauce should work. If the recipe calls for more than ½ cup oil, then experiment with half oil, half applesauce. You've still made the recipe healthier, even if you haven't removed all the oil from it.

Another rule for healthy substitution: up to ½ cup of sugar or less can be replaced by *an artificial sweetener* (like Sugar Twin or Sprinkle Sweet) *that can withstand the heat of baking.* If it requires more than ½ cup sugar, cut the amount needed by 75 percent and use ½ cup sugar substitute and sugar for the rest. Other options: reduce the butter and sugar by 25 percent and see if the finished product still satisfies you in taste and appearance. Or, make the cookies just the way Grandma did, realizing they are part of your family's holiday tradition. Enjoy a moderate serving of a couple of cookies once or twice during the season, and just forget about them the rest of the year.

I'm sure you'll add to this list of cooking tips as you begin preparing Healthy Exchanges recipes and discover how easy it can be to adapt your own favorite recipes using these ideas and your own common sense.

A Peek Into My Pantry and My Favorite Brands

Everyone asks me what foods I keep on hand and what brands I use. There are lots of good products on the grocery shelves today—many more than we dreamed about even a year or two ago. And I can't wait to see what's out there twelve months from now. The following are my staples and, where appropriate, my favorites *at this time*. I feel these products are healthier, tastier, easy to get—and deliver the most flavor for the least amount of fat, sugar, or calories. If you find others you like as well *or better*, please use them. This is only a guide to make your grocery shopping and cooking easier.

Fat-free plain yogurt (*Yoplait*)
Nonfat dry skim milk powder (*Carnation*)
Evaporated skim milk (*Carnation*)
Skim milk
Fat-free cottage cheese
Fat-free cream cheese (*Philadelphia*)
Fat-free mayonnaise (*Kraft*)
Fat-free salad dressings (*Kraft*)
Fat-free sour cream (*Land O Lakes*)
Reduced-calorie margarine (*Weight Watchers, Promise, or Smart Beat*)
Cooking spray:
 Olive oil–flavored and regular (*Pam*)

Butter flavored for sautéing (*Weight Watchers*)

Butter flavored for spritzing *after* cooking (*I Can't Believe It's Not Butter!*)

Vegetable oil (*Puritan Canola Oil*)

Reduced-calorie whipped topping (*Cool Whip Lite*)

Sugar Substitute:

If no heating is involved (*Equal*)

If heating is required:

white (*Sugar Twin or Sprinkle Sweet*)

brown (*Brown Sugar Twin*)

Sugar-free gelatin and pudding mixes (*JELL-O*)

Baking mix (*Bisquick Reduced-Fat*)

Pancake mix (*Aunt Jemima Reduced Calorie*)

Reduced-calorie pancake syrup (*Cary's Sugar Free*)

Parmesan cheese (*Kraft Fat Free or Weight Watchers Fat Free*)

Reduced-fat cheese (*Kraft ⅓ Less Fat and Weight Watchers*)

Shredded frozen potatoes (*Mr. Dell's*)

Spreadable fruit spread (*Smucker's, Welch's or Sorrell Ridge*)

Peanut butter (*Peter Pan Reduced Fat, Jif Reduced Fat, or Skippy Reduced Fat*)

Chicken broth (*Healthy Request*)

Beef broth (*Swanson*)

Tomato sauce (*Hunts—Chunky and Regular*)

Canned soups (*Healthy Request*)

Tomato juice (*Campbell's Reduced Sodium*)

Ketchup (*Heinz Lite Harvest or Healthy Choice*)

Purchased piecrust:

unbaked (*Pillsbury—from dairy case*)

graham cracker, butter flavored, or chocolate flavored (*Keebler*)

Pastrami and corned beef (*Carl Buddig Lean*)

Luncheon meats (*Healthy Choice or Oscar Mayer*)

Ham (*Dubuque 97% fat free and reduced sodium or Healthy Choice*)

Frankfurters and Kielbasa sausage (*Healthy Choice*)

Canned white chicken, packed in water (*Swanson*)

Canned tuna, packed in water (*Starkist*)

90-percent-lean ground turkey and beef

Soda crackers (*Nabisco Fat Free*)

Reduced-calorie bread—40 calories per slice or less

Hamburger buns—80 calories each (*Colonial Old Fashion or Less*)

Rice—instant, regular, brown, and wild

Instant potato flakes (*Betty Crocker Potato Buds*)

Noodles, spaghetti, and macaroni

Salsa (*Chi-Chi's Mild*)

Pickle relish—dill, sweet, and hot dog

Mustard—Dijon, prepared, and spicy

Unsweetened apple juice

Unsweetened applesauce

Fruit—fresh, frozen (no sugar added), or canned in juice

Vegetables—fresh, frozen, or canned

Spices—JO's Spices

Lemon and lime juice (in small plastic fruit-shaped bottles found in produce section)

Instant fruit beverage mixes (*Crystal Light*)

Dry dairy beverage mixes (*Nestlé's Quik and Swiss Miss*)

"Ice cream"—*Well's Blue Bunny Health Beat Fat and Sugar Free*

The items on my shopping list are everyday foods found in just about any grocery store in America. But all are as low in fat, sugar, calories, and sodium as I can find—and that still taste good! I can make any recipe in my cookbooks and newsletters as long as I have my cupboards and refrigerator stocked with these items. Whenever I use the last of any one item, I just make sure I pick up another supply the next time I'm at the store.

If your grocer does not stock these items, why not ask if they can be ordered on a trial basis? If the store agrees to do so, be sure to tell your friends to stop by, so that sales are good enough to warrant restocking the new products. Competition for shelf space is fierce, so only products that sell well stay around.

Shopping the Healthy Exchanges Way

Sometimes, as part of a cooking demonstration, I take the group on a field trip to the nearest supermarket. There's no better place to share my discoveries about which healthy products taste best, which are best for you, and which healthy products don't deliver enough taste to include in my recipes.

While I'd certainly enjoy accompanying you to your neighborhood store, we'll have to settle for a field trip *on paper*. I've tasted and tried just about every fat- and sugar-free product on the market, but so many new ones keep coming out all the time, you're going to have to learn to play detective on your own. I've turned label reading into an art, but often the label doesn't tell me everything I need to know.

Sometimes you'll find, as I have, that the product with *no* fat doesn't provide the taste satisfaction you require; other times, a no-fat or low-fat product just doesn't cook up the same way as the original product. And some foods, including even the leanest meats, can't eliminate *all* the fat. That's okay, though—a healthy diet should include anywhere from 15 to 25 percent of total calories from fat on any given day.

Take my word for it—your supermarket is filled with lots of delicious foods that can and should be part of your healthy diet for life. Come, join me as we check it out on the way to the checkout!

First stop, the **salad dressing** aisle. Salad dressing is usually a high-fat food, but there are great alternatives available. Let's look first at the regular Ranch dressing—2 tablespoons have 170 calories and 18 grams of fat—and who can eat just 2 tablespoons? Already, that's about half the fat grams most people should consume in a day. Of course, it's the most flavorful too. Now let's look at the low-fat version. Two tablespoons have 110 calories and 11 grams of fat; they took about half of the fat out, but there's still a lot of sugar there. The fat-free version has 50 calories and zero grams of fat, but they also took most of the flavor out. Here's what you do to get it back: add a tablespoon of fat-free mayonnaise, a few more parsley flakes, and about a half teaspoon of sugar substitute to your two-tablespoon serving. That trick, with the fat-free mayo and sugar substitute, will work with just about any fat-free dressing and give it more of that full-bodied flavor of the high-fat version. Be careful not to add too much sugar substitute—you don't want it to become sickeningly sweet.

I even use Kraft fat-free **mayonnaise** at 10 calories per tablespoon to make scalloped potatoes. The Smart Beat brand is also a good one.

Before I buy anything at the store, I read the label carefully: the total fat plus the saturated fat; I look to see how many calories are in a realistic serving, and I say to myself, would I eat that much—or would I eat more? I look at the sodium and I look at the total carbohydrates. I like to check those ingredients because I'm cooking for diabetics and heart patients, too. And I check the total calories from fat.

Remember that 1 fat gram equals 9 calories, while 1 protein or 1 carbohydrate gram equals 4 calories.

A wonderful new product is I Can't Believe It's Not Butter! spray, with zero calories and zero grams of fat in four squirts. It's great for your air-popped popcorn. As for **light margarine spread**, beware—most of the fat-free brands don't melt on toast, and they don't taste very good either, so I just leave them on the shelf. For the few times I do use a light margarine I tend to buy Smart Beat Ultra, Promise Ultra, or Weight Watchers Light Ultra. The number-one ingredient in them is water. I occasionally use the light margarine in cooking, but I don't really put margarine on my toast anymore. I use apple butter or make a spread with fat-free cream cheese mixed with a little spreadable fruit instead.

So far, Pillsbury hasn't released a reduced-fat **crescent roll**, so you'll only get one crescent roll per serving from me. I usually make eight of the rolls serve twelve by using them for a crust. The house brands may be lower in fat but they're usually not as good flavor-wise—and don't quite cover the pan when you use them to make a crust. If you're going to use crescent rolls with lots of other stuff on top, then a house brand might be fine.

The Pillsbury French Loaf makes a wonderful **pizza crust** and fills a giant jelly roll pan. One-fifth of this package "costs" you only 1 gram of fat (and I don't even let you have that much). Once you use this for your pizza crust, you will never go back to anything else instead. I use it to make calzones too.

I only use Philadelphia Fat Free **cream cheese** because it has the best consistency. I've tried other brands, but I wasn't happy with them. Healthy Choice makes lots of great products, but their cream cheese just doesn't work as well with my recipes.

Let's move to the **cheese** aisle. My preferred brand is Kraft ⅓ less fat shredded cheese. I will not use the fat-free versions because *they don't melt.* I would gladly give up sugar and fat, but I will not give up flavor. This is a happy compromise. I use the reduced-fat version. I use less, and I use it where your eyes "eat" it, on top of the recipe. So you walk away satisfied and with a finished product that's very low in fat. If you want to make grilled-cheese sandwiches for your kids, use the Kraft ⅓ less fat cheese slices, and it'll taste exactly like the one they're used to. The fat-free will not.

Some brands have come out with a fat-free **hot dog**, but the ones we've tasted haven't been very good. So far, among the low-fat brands, I think Healthy Choice tastes the best. Did you know that regular hot dogs have as many as 15 grams of fat?

Dubuque's extra-lean reduced-sodium **ham** tastes wonderful, reduces the sodium as well as the fat, and gives you a larger serving. Don't be fooled by products called turkey ham; they may *not* be lower in fat than a very lean pork product. Here's one label as an example: I checked a brand of turkey ham called Genoa. It gives you a 2-ounce serving for 70 calories and 3½ grams of fat. The Dubuque extra-lean ham, made from pork, gives you a 3-ounce serving for 90 calories, but only 2½ grams of fat. *You get more food and less fat.*

The same can be true of packaged **ground turkey**; if you're not buying *fresh* ground turkey, you may be getting a product with turkey skin and a lot of fat ground up in it. Look to be sure the package is labeled with the fat content; if it isn't, run the other way!

Your best bets in **snack foods** are pretzels, which are always low in fat, as well as the chips from the Guiltless Gourmet, which taste especially good with one of my dips.

Frozen dinners can be expensive and high in sodium, but it's smart to have two or three in the freezer as a backup when your best-laid plans go awry and you need to grab something on the run. It's not a good idea to rely on them too much—what if you can't get to the store to get them, or you're short on cash? The sodium can be high in some of them because they often replace the fat with salt, so do read the labels. Also ask yourself if the serving is enough to satisfy you; for many of us, it's not.

Egg substitute is expensive, and probably not necessary unless you're cooking for someone who has to worry about every bit of cholesterol in his or her diet. If you occasionally have a fried egg or an omelet, *use the real egg*. For cooking, you can usually substitute two egg whites for one whole egg. Most of the time it won't make any difference, but check your recipe carefully.

Frozen pizzas aren't particularly healthy, but used occasionally, in moderation, they're okay. Your best bet is to make your own using the Pillsbury French Crust. Take a look at the frozen pizza package of your choice, though, because you may find that plain cheese pizza, which you might think would be the healthiest, might actually have the most fat. Since there's nothing else on there, they have to cover the crust with a heavy layer of high-fat cheese. A veggie pizza generally uses less cheese and more healthy, crunchy vegetables.

Healthy frozen desserts are hard to find except for the Weight Watchers brands. I've always felt that their portions are so small, and for their size still pretty high in fat and sugar. (This is one of the reasons I think I'll be successful marketing my frozen desserts someday.) Keep an eye out for fat-free or very low-fat frozen yogurt or sorbet products. Even Häagen-Dazs, which makes some of the highest-fat-content ice cream, now has a fat-free fruit sorbet pop out that's pretty good. I'm sure there will be more before too long.

You have to be realistic: What are you willing to do, and what are you *not* willing to do? Let's take bread, for example. Some people just have to have the real thing—rye bread with caraway seeds or a whole-wheat version with bits of bran in it.

I prefer to use reduced-calorie **bread** because I like a *real* sandwich. This way, I can have two slices of bread and it counts as only one bread/starch exchange.

Do you love **croutons**? Forget the ones from the grocery store—they're extremely high in fat. Instead, take reduced-calorie bread, toast it, give it a quick spray of I Can't Believe It's Not Butter! spray, and let it dry a bit. Cut the bread in cubes. Then, for an extra-good flavor, put the pieces in a plastic bag with a couple of tablespoons of grated Kraft fat-free Parmesan cheese and shake them up. You might be surprised just how good they are. Here's another product that's really good for croutons—Corn Chex cereal. Sprinkle a few Chex on top of your salad, and I think you'll be pleasantly surprised. I've also found that Rice Chex, crushed up, with parsley flakes and a little bit of Parmesan cheese, makes a great topping for casseroles that you used to put potato chips on.

Salad toppers can make a lot of difference in how content you feel after you've eaten. Some low-fat cheese, some homemade croutons, and even some bacon bits on top of your greens deliver an abundance of tasty satisfaction. I always use the real Hormel **bacon bits** instead of the imitation bacon-flavored bits. I only use a small amount, but you get that real bacon flavor—and less fat, too.

How I Shop

I always keep my kitchen stocked with my basic staples; that way, I can go to the cupboard and create new recipes anytime I'm inspired. I hope you will take the time (and allot the money) to stock your cupboards with items from the staples list, so you can enjoy developing your own healthy versions of family favorites without making extra trips to the market.

I'm always on the lookout for new products sitting on the grocery shelf. When I spot something I haven't seen before, I'll usually grab it, glance at the front, then turn it around and read the label carefully. I call it looking at the promises (the "come-on" on the front of the package) and then at the warranty (the ingredients list and the label on the back).

If it looks as good on the back as it does on the front, I'll say okay and either create a recipe on the spot or take it home for when I do think of something to do with it. Picking up a new product is just about the only time I buy something not on my list.

The items on my shopping list are normal, everyday foods, but as low-fat and low-sugar (*while still tasting good*) as I can find. I can make any recipe in this book as long as these staples are on my shelves. After using these products for a couple of weeks, you will find it becomes routine to have them on hand. And I promise you, I really don't spend any more at the store now than I did a few years ago when I told myself I couldn't afford some of these items. Back then, of course, plenty of unhealthy, high-priced snacks I really didn't need somehow made the magic leap from the grocery shelves into my cart. Who was I kidding?

Yes, you often have to pay a little more for fat-free or low-fat products, including meats. But since I frequently use a half pound of meat to serve four to six people, your cost per serving will be much lower.

Try adding up what you were spending before on chips and cookies, premium brand ice cream and fatty cuts of meat, and you'll soon see that we've *streamlined* your shopping cart—and taken the weight off your pocketbook as well as your hips!

Remember, your good health is *your* business—but it's big business, too. Write to the manufacturers of products you and your family enjoy but feel are just too high in fat, sugar, or sodium to be part of your new healthy lifestyle. Companies are spending millions of dollars to respond to consumers' concerns about food products, and I bet that in the next few years, you'll discover fat-free and low-fat versions of nearly every product piled high on your supermarket shelves!

The Healthy

Exchanges Kitchen

You might be surprised to discover I still don't have a massive test kitchen stocked with every modern appliance and handy gadget ever made. The tiny galley kitchen where I first launched Healthy Exchanges has room for only one person at a time in it, but that never stopped me from feeling the sky's the limit when it comes to seeking out great healthy taste!

Because storage is at such a premium in my kitchen, I don't waste space with equipment I don't really need. Here's a list of what I consider worth having. If you notice serious gaps in your equipment, you can probably find most of what you need at a local discount store or garage sale. If your kitchen is equipped with more sophisticated appliances, don't feel guilty about using them. Enjoy every appliance you can find room for or that you can afford. Just be assured that healthy, quick, and delicious food can be prepared with the "basics."

A Healthy Exchanges
Kitchen Equipment List

Good-quality nonstick skillets (medium, large)
Good-quality saucepans (small, medium, large)
Glass mixing bowls (small, medium, large)
Glass measures (1-cup, 2-cup, 4-cup, 8-cup)
Sharp knives (paring, chef, butcher)
Rubber spatulas
Wire whisks
Measuring spoons
Large mixing spoons
Egg separator
Covered jar
Vegetable parer
Grater
Potato masher
Electric mixer
Electric blender
Electric skillet
Cooking timer
Slow cooker
Air popper for popcorn
4-inch round custard dishes
Glass pie plates
8-by-8-inch glass baking dishes
Cake pans (9-by-9, 9-by-13-inch)
10¾-by-7-by-1½-inch biscuit pan
Cookie sheets (good nonstick ones)
Jelly roll pan
Muffin tins
5-by-9-inch bread pan
Plastic colander
Cutting board
Pie wedge server
Square-shaped server
Can opener (I prefer manual)

Rolling pin

Kitchen scales (unless you *always* use my recipes)

Wire racks for cooling baked goods

Electric toaster oven (to conserve energy for those times when only one item is being baked or for a recipe that calls for a short baking time)

How to Read a Healthy Exchanges Recipe

The Healthy Exchanges Nutritional Analysis

Before using these recipes, you may wish to consult your physician or health-care provider to be sure they are appropriate for you. The information in this book is not intended to take the place of any medical advice. It reflects my experiences, studies, research, and opinions regarding healthy eating.

Each recipe includes nutritional information calculated in three ways:

> Healthy Exchanges Weight Loss Choices or Exchanges
> Calories, fiber, and fat grams
> Diabetic exchanges

In every Healthy Exchanges recipe, the diabetic exchanges have been calculated by a registered dietitian. All the other calculations were done by computer, using the Food Processor II software. When the ingredient listing gives more than one choice, the first ingredient listed is the one used in the recipe analysis. Due to inevitable variations in the ingredients you choose to use, the nutritional values should be considered approximate.

The annotation "(limited)" following Protein counts in some

recipes indicates that consumption of whole eggs should be limited to four per week.

Please note the following symbols:

☆ This star means read the recipe's directions carefully for special instructions about **division** of ingredients.

✳ This symbol indicates **FREEZES WELL.**

A Few Cooking Terms to Ease the Way

Everyone can learn to cook *The Healthy Exchanges Way*. It's simple, it's quick, and the results are delicious! If you've tended to avoid the kitchen because you find recipe instructions confusing or complicated, I hope I can help you feel more confident. I'm not offering a full cooking course here, just some terms I use often that I know you'll want to understand.

Bake: To cook food in the oven; sometimes called roasting

Beat: To mix very fast with a spoon, wire whisk, or electric mixer

Blend: To mix two or more ingredients together thoroughly so that the mixture is smooth

Boil: To cook in liquid until bubbles form

Brown: To cook at low to medium-low heat until ingredients turn brown

Chop: To cut food into small pieces with a knife, blender, or food processor

Cool: To let stand at room temperature until food is no longer hot to the touch

Combine: To mix ingredients together with a spoon

Dice:	To chop into small, even-sized pieces
Drain:	To pour off liquid; sometimes you will need to reserve the liquid to use in the recipe, so please read carefully
Drizzle:	To sprinkle drops of liquid (for example, chocolate syrup) lightly over top of food
Fold in:	To combine delicate ingredients with other foods by using a gentle, circular motion. Example: adding Cool Whip Lite to an already stirred-up bowl of pudding
Preheat:	To heat your oven to the desired temperature, usually about ten minutes before you put your food in to bake
Sauté:	To cook in a skillet or frying pan until food is soft
Simmer:	To cook in a small amount of liquid over low heat; this lets the flavors blend without too much liquid evaporating
Whisk:	To beat with a wire whisk until mixture is well mixed; don't worry about finesse here, just use some elbow grease!

How to Measure

I try to make it as easy as possible by providing more than one measurement for many ingredients in my recipes—both the weight in ounces and the amount measured by a measuring cup, for example. Just remember:

- You measure **solids** (flour, Cool Whip Lite, yogurt, macaroni, nonfat dry milk powder) in your set of separate measuring cups (¼, ⅓, ½, 1 cup)

- You measure **liquids** (Diet Mountain Dew, water, tomato juice) in the clear glass or plastic measuring cups that measure ounces, cups, and pints. Set the cup on a level surface and pour the liquid into it, or you may get too much.

- You can use your measuring spoon set for liquids or solids. **Note:** Don't pour a liquid like an extract into a measuring spoon held over the bowl and run the risk of overpouring; instead, do it over the sink.

Here are a few handy equivalents:

3 teaspoons	equal	1 tablespoon
4 tablespoons	equal	¼ cup
5⅓ tablespoons	equal	⅓ cup
8 tablespoons	equal	½ cup
10⅔ tablespoons	equal	⅔ cup
12 tablespoons	equal	¾ cup
16 tablespoons	equal	1 cup
2 cups	equal	1 pint
4 cups	equal	1 quart
8 ounces liquid	equal	1 fluid cup

That's it. Now, ready, set, cook!

In the Microwave

Can you remember a time when your kitchen didn't include this handiest of appliances? Do you recall when baking a potato took an hour in a traditional oven? Or when frozen dinners required 45 minutes to heat up and turned your kitchen into a sauna in the warmer months?

As a working woman and a mother, I welcomed the ease and speed of microwave cooking, but I soon learned that actually using this "miracle method" required careful testing to find just the right combination of solid and liquid ingredients, the ideal bowl or pan, and the perfect amount of time to produce a delicious result.

I've done all the hard work—now the easy stuff is up to you. These delectable recipes require minimal work and deliver maximum flavor, all while keeping the fat and sugar low.

Keep in mind: Just as every conventional oven differs in its distribution of heat, so does every microwave, depending on wattage, size, and special features like a carousel. My recipes have been calculated for a standard 900-watt midsized oven. If yours is smaller or larger, less or more powerful, check your dish after cooking it for 75 percent of the recommended time.

In the Microwave

French Onion and Beef Soup

Traditional French onion soup boasts the rich flavor of onions and cheese in a hearty beef broth, but this recipe takes it one better by adding chunks of roast beef to the blend. If you're looking for a soup filling enough all by itself for a meal, this is the one!

○ Serves 4 (1 cup)

1¾ cups (one 15-ounce can) Swanson Beef Broth

2 cups water

1 teaspoon Worcestershire sauce

4 cups thinly sliced onion

1 full cup (6 ounces) diced lean cooked roast beef

4 slices reduced-calorie French bread, toasted and cubed

4 (¾-ounce) slices Kraft reduced-fat Swiss cheese

In an 8-cup glass measuring bowl, combine beef broth, water, Worcestershire sauce, and onion. Cover and microwave on HIGH (100% power) for 15 minutes, stirring after every 5 minutes. Stir in beef. Re-cover and continue microwaving on HIGH for 5 minutes. Evenly sprinkle toasted bread cubes over soup and arrange cheese slice over top. Microwave on HIGH for 1 to 2 minutes or until cheese melts. Serve at once.

HINT: If you don't have leftovers, purchase a chunk of cooked roast beef from your local deli *or* use Healthy Choice Deli slices, chopped. Either works great.

Each serving equals:

HE: 2 Protein • 2 Vegetable • ½ Bread •
18 Optional Calories

225 Calories • 5 gm Fat • 24 gm Protein •
21 gm Carbohydrate • 552 mg Sodium • 3 gm Fiber

DIABETIC: 2 Meat • 1 Vegetable • 1 Starch

Lazy Day Chili

Have you ever used your microwave to brown meat or sauté onions? It's simpler than you might think, and great for good-health eating because it removes so much fat from the dish! This chili dish is so substantial, you'll feel warm, cozy, and satisfied all the way to your toes!   ❍   Serves 4 (1½ cups)

> 8 ounces ground 90% lean turkey or beef
> ½ cup chopped onion
> 1¾ cups (one 15-ounce can) Hunt's Chunky Tomato Sauce
> ½ cup (one 2.5-ounce jar) sliced mushrooms, drained
> 1¾ cups (one 15-ounce can) Swanson Beef Broth
> 10 ounces (one 16-ounce can) red kidney beans, rinsed and
>   drained
> 2 teaspoons chili seasoning mix
> ¼ teaspoon black pepper
> Scant ½ cup (¾ ounce) Corn Chex, slightly crushed

Place meat and onion in a plastic colander and set colander in a 9-inch glass pie plate. Microwave on HIGH (100% power) for 3 to 4 minutes, or until meat is browned, stirring after 2 minutes. In an 8-cup glass measuring bowl, combine browned meat mixture, tomato sauce, mushrooms, and beef broth. Add kidney beans, chili seasoning mix, and black pepper. Mix well to combine. Cover and continue microwaving on MEDIUM (50% power) for 15 minutes, turning and stirring after 6 minutes. When serving, garnish each bowl with 2 tablespoons crushed Corn Chex.

Each serving equals:

HE: 2¾ Protein • 2¼ Vegetable • ¼ Bread •
9 Optional Calories

201 Calories • 5 gm Fat • 17 gm Protein •
22 gm Carbohydrate • 947 mg Sodium • 5 gm Fiber

DIABETIC: 2 Meat • 1½ Starch • 1 Vegetable *or*
2 Meat • 1 Carbohydrate

Zucchini-Tomato Bake

Fresh vegetables keep their shape and flavor so well in the microwave, and their natural moisture provides most of the liquid to bake the dish to perfection. The fragrance of basil will escape just enough to perfume your kitchen with the scent of culinary pleasure!

○ Serves 4

> 2 cups sliced zucchini☆
> 2 cups sliced fresh tomatoes☆
> ½ cup chopped onion☆
> 1 tablespoon fresh chopped basil or 1 teaspoon dried basil☆
> ¾ cup (3 ounces) shredded Kraft reduced-fat mozzarella cheese☆

In an 8-by-8-inch glass microwavable baking dish sprayed with butter-flavored cooking spray, layer 1 cup zucchini, 1 cup sliced tomatoes, and ¼ cup chopped onion. Evenly sprinkle basil and ½ cup mozzarella cheese over top. Repeat layers with remaining zucchini, tomatoes, onion, and mozzarella cheese. Cover and microwave on HIGH (100% power) for 10 minutes, turning dish after 5 minutes. Continue microwaving on BAKE (60% power) for 10 minutes. Place baking dish on a wire rack and let set for 5 minutes. Divide into 4 servings.

Each serving equals:

HE: 2¼ Vegetable • 1 Protein

91 Calories • 3 gm Fat • 8 gm Protein •
8 gm Carbohydrate • 230 mg Sodium • 2 gm Fiber

DIABETIC: 2 Vegetable • 1 Meat

Pasta Roma

This creamy, speedy pasta preparation is extra-nutritious with the addition of the dry milk powder—and it's also extra smooooooth! I always suggest making more pasta than you require for the recipe you're making, dividing it into two-cup portions, and freezing or refrigerating for later use. ❂ Serves 4 (full ¾ cup)

> *1 cup (one 8-ounce can) Hunt's Tomato Sauce*
> *⅓ cup Carnation Nonfat Dry Milk Powder*
> *½ cup (one 2.5-ounce jar) sliced mushrooms, drained*
> *1 teaspoon Italian seasoning*
> *¼ teaspoon black pepper*
> *1 teaspoon Sugar Twin or Sprinkle Sweet*
> *½ cup frozen peas*
> *2 cups hot cooked rotini pasta, rinsed and drained*

In an 8-cup glass measuring bowl, combine tomato sauce and dry milk powder. Add mushrooms, Italian seasoning, black pepper, and Sugar Twin. Mix well to combine. Cover and microwave on HIGH (100% power) for 2 minutes. Stir in peas and rotini pasta. Continue microwaving on HIGH for 4 minutes, stirring after 2 minutes. Place bowl on a wire rack and let set for 2 or 3 minutes. Mix well before serving.

HINT: 1½ cups uncooked rotini pasta usually cooks to about 2 cups.

Each serving equals:

HE: 1¼ Bread • 1¼ Vegetable • ¼ Skim Milk • 1 Optional Calorie

153 Calories • 1 gm Fat • 7 gm Protein • 29 gm Carbohydrate • 516 mg Sodium • 2 gm Fiber

DIABETIC: 1½ Starch • 1 Vegetable

Quick Pizza Potato Hash

If your family loves potatoes as much as Cliff does, you're going to adore this fun and flavorful potato "pizza" dish! The shredded potatoes form a delectable crust, and it's so easy to make, your teenagers may start stirring it up themselves for parties.

● Serves 4

> 3½ cups (15 ounces) shredded frozen potatoes, slightly thawed
>
> 1 cup (one 8-ounce can) Hunt's Tomato Sauce
>
> 1 teaspoon Italian seasoning
>
> ½ cup (one 2.5-ounce jar) sliced mushrooms, drained
>
> ¼ cup (1 ounce) sliced ripe olives
>
> ¾ cup (3 ounces) shredded Kraft reduced-fat mozzarella cheese

Place potatoes in a 9-inch glass pie plate. Cover and microwave on HIGH (100% power) for 7 to 8 minutes, turning pie plate after 4 minutes. In a medium bowl, combine tomato sauce, Italian seasoning, mushrooms, and olives. Spoon sauce mixture evenly over potatoes. Evenly sprinkle mozzarella cheese over top. Microwave on HIGH for 3 to 4 minutes or until cheese melts, turning pie plate after 2 minutes.

HINTS: 1. Mr. Dell's shredded potatoes work great.

2. Raw shredded potatoes may be used in place of purchased frozen ones.

Each serving equals:

HE: 1¼ Vegetable • 1 Protein • ¾ Bread • ¼ Fat

168 Calories • 4 gm Fat • 10 gm Protein •
23 gm Carbohydrate • 726 mg Sodium • 3 gm Fiber

DIABETIC: 1 Vegetable • 1 Meat • 1 Starch

Chicken à la Rice

Inspired by that old-time classic, Chicken à la King, here's a super-fast version that sparkles with bits of red (pimiento) and green (peas) for a lovely holiday dish! Instead of serving this luscious concoction over the traditional noodles, I mixed up some handy rice. Surprise—instant goodness, courtesy of those mysterious microwaves!   ◐   Serves 4 (1 full cup)

1 (10¾-ounce) can Healthy Request Cream of Chicken Soup

1 cup water

⅓ cup Carnation Nonfat Dry Milk Powder

1 cup (5 ounces) diced cooked chicken breast

½ cup (one 2.5-ounce jar) sliced mushrooms, drained

2 tablespoons canned chopped pimientos

½ cup frozen peas

⅛ teaspoon black pepper

⅔ cup (2 ounces) uncooked instant rice

1 hard-boiled egg, chopped

In an 8-cup glass measuring bowl, combine chicken soup, water, and dry milk powder. Add chicken, mushrooms, pimientos, peas, and black pepper. Mix well to combine. Cover and microwave on HIGH (100% power) for 5 minutes. Stir in uncooked rice. Re-cover and let set for 5 minutes. Add egg. Mix gently before serving. Serve at once.

HINTS: 1. If you don't have leftovers, purchase a chunk of cooked chicken breast from your local deli.

2. If you want the look and feel of eggs without the cholesterol, toss out the yolk and dice the whites.

Each serving equals:

HE: 1½ Protein (¼ limited) • ¾ Bread • ¼ Skim Milk • ¼ Vegetable • ½ Slider • 5 Optional Calories

200 Calories • 4 gm Fat • 18 gm Protein • 23 gm Carbohydrate • 490 mg Sodium • 2 gm Fiber

DIABETIC: 2 Meat • 1½ Starch

Tuna Potato Dish with Corn Topping

Here's a recipe full of taste surprises that is sure to win smiles all around! The bottom part is a kind of tuna-flavored shepherd's pie (with all those cozy mashed potatoes); the topping of cheese and corn is almost too good to be true—*and* healthy!

○ Serves 4

> 1²⁄₃ cups water
> 1¹⁄₃ cups (3 ounces) instant potato flakes
> ¹⁄₃ cup Carnation Nonfat Dry Milk Powder
> ¹⁄₄ cup Kraft fat-free mayonnaise
> ¹⁄₄ teaspoon black pepper
> 1 teaspoon dried onion flakes
> 1 teaspoon dried parsley flakes
> 1 teaspoon chili seasoning mix
> 1 (6-ounce) can white tuna, packed in water,
>   drained and flaked
> 1 cup (one 8-ounce can) cream-style corn
> ¾ cup (3 ounces) shredded Kraft reduced-fat
>   Cheddar cheese

Spray an 8-by-8-inch glass microwavable baking dish with butter-flavored cooking spray. In an 8-cup glass measuring bowl, microwave water on HIGH (100% power) for 2 minutes or until water starts to boil. Add potato flakes and dry milk powder. Mix well to combine. Let set for 2 to 3 minutes. Stir in mayonnaise, black pepper, onion flakes, parsley flakes, and chili seasoning mix. Add tuna. Mix well to combine. Spread mixture into prepared baking dish. In a small bowl, combine corn and Cheddar cheese. Evenly spread corn mixture over top of tuna mixture. Microwave on HIGH for 8 minutes, turning dish after 4 minutes. Place baking dish on a wire rack and let set for 3 minutes. Divide into 4 servings.

Each serving equals:

HE: 1¾ Protein • 1½ Bread • ¼ Skim Milk • 10 Optional Calories

252 Calories • 4 gm Fat • 22 gm Protein • 32 gm Carbohydrate • 650 mg Sodium • 2 gm Fiber

DIABETIC: 3 Meat • 2 Starch

Roman Tuna and Noodles

I get lots of requests for easy tuna suppers, in part because so many people love the taste of tuna, but also because it's a great, inexpensive source of good-for-you protein! Here's a luscious blend of homemade creamy flavor inspired by the tangy flavors of Italy. The Parmesan cheese will fill your house with a delectable aroma.

○ Serves 4 (1½ cups)

> 2 teaspoons reduced-calorie margarine
> ¾ cup thinly sliced onion
> 1 teaspoon dried minced garlic
> 1 (10¾-ounce) can Healthy Request Cream of Mushroom Soup
> 1¾ cups (one 14½-ounce can) stewed tomatoes, undrained
> 1 teaspoon Italian seasoning
> 2 cups hot cooked noodles, rinsed and drained
> 1 (6-ounce) can white tuna, packed in water, drained and flaked
> ¼ cup (¾ ounce) grated Kraft fat-free Parmesan cheese

In an 8-cup glass measuring bowl, combine margarine, onion, and garlic. Microwave on HIGH (100% power) for 2 minutes. Add mushroom soup, undrained stewed tomatoes, and Italian seasoning. Mix well to combine. Cover and continue microwaving on HIGH for 4 to 5 minutes, stirring after 2 minutes. Add noodles, tuna, and Parmesan cheese. Mix well to combine. Microwave on HIGH for 3 to 4 minutes, stirring after 2 minutes. Place bowl on a wire rack and let set for 2 to 3 minutes. Mix gently before serving.

HINT: 1¾ cups uncooked noodles usually cooks to about 2 cups.

Each serving equals:

> HE: 1¼ Vegetable • 1 Bread • 1 Protein • ¼ Fat •
> ½ Slider • 1 Optional Calorie
>
> ---
>
> 227 Calories • 3 gm Fat • 18 gm Protein •
> 32 gm Carbohydrate • 560 mg Sodium • 2 gm Fiber
>
> ---
>
> DIABETIC: 2 Meat • 1½ Starch • 1 Vegetable

Pizza Hot Dish

If you like to nibble the toppings off a piece of takeout pizza, you'll enjoy this hot noodle dish—it's *ALL* toppings! In fact, it's so full of the flavors of pizza, you're bound to start looking for the crust!

● Serves 4 (scant 1 cup)

> 8 ounces ground 90% lean turkey or beef
>
> 1¾ cups (3 ounces) uncooked noodles
>
> 1¾ cups (one 15-ounce can) Hunt's Chunky Tomato Sauce
>
> 1 teaspoon pizza seasoning or Italian seasoning
>
> 1 teaspoon Sugar Twin or Sprinkle Sweet
>
> ½ cup (one 2.5-ounce jar) sliced mushrooms, undrained
>
> Full ½ cup (2¼ ounces) shredded Kraft reduced-fat mozzarella
> cheese

Place meat in a plastic colander and set colander in a 9-inch glass pie plate. Microwave on HIGH (100% power) for 3 to 4 minutes, or until meat is browned, stirring after 2 minutes. In an 8-cup glass measuring bowl, combine browned meat and uncooked noodles. In a medium bowl, combine tomato sauce, pizza seasoning, Sugar Twin, and mushrooms. Add sauce mixture to meat mixture. Mix well to combine. Cover and vent one corner. Microwave on HIGH for 10 minutes. Stir in mozzarella cheese. Re-cover and continue microwaving on HIGH for 2 minutes or until noodles are tender and cheese is melted. Place bowl on a wire rack and let set for 5 minutes. Mix well before serving.

Each serving equals:

HE: 2½ Protein • 2 Vegetable • 1 Bread

244 Calories • 8 gm Fat • 19 gm Protein •
24 gm Carbohydrate • 926 mg Sodium • 1 gm Fiber

DIABETIC: 2½ Meat • 2 Vegetable • 1 Starch

Lasagna Casserole

I'll bet you love the taste of lasagna, but you've always thought that preparing your own at home was too much trouble. This recipe was designed to change your mind forever! Once you've used the microwave to brown the meat, it's all in the layering. This one takes a bit more time than some other dishes in this section, but the finished dish is dazzling! (And the good news is, it serves eight, so you're almost bound to have leftovers!) ☻ Serves 8

> 8 ounces ground 90% lean turkey or beef
> ¼ cup chopped onion
> 1¾ cups (one 14½-ounce can) Italian stewed tomatoes, coarsely
>   chopped and undrained
> 2 cups (two 8-ounce cans) Hunt's Tomato Sauce
> 1 teaspoon Italian seasoning
> 2 cups fat-free cottage cheese
> ¼ cup (¾ ounce) grated Kraft fat-free Parmesan cheese
> 1 egg, slightly beaten, or equivalent in egg substitute
> 1 tablespoon dried parsley flakes
> 6 uncooked lasagna noodles
> 1½ cups (6 ounces) shredded Kraft reduced-fat mozzarella
>   cheese

Spray a 9-by-13-inch glass microwavable baking dish with olive oil–flavored cooking spray. Place meat and onion in a plastic colander and set colander in a 9-inch glass pie plate. Microwave on HIGH (100% power) for 3 to 4 minutes, or until meat is browned, stirring after 2 minutes. In a medium bowl, combine browned meat, undrained stewed tomatoes, tomato sauce, and Italian seasoning. In another medium bowl, combine cottage cheese, Parmesan cheese, egg, and parsley flakes. In prepared baking dish, layer 1 cup meat sauce, 3 uncooked noodles, ½ of cottage cheese mixture, and ¾ cup mozzarella cheese. Repeat layers, starting with 1 cup meat sauce. Spread all remaining meat sauce over top. Cover and microwave on HIGH for 15 minutes. Turn dish. Continue microwaving on MEDIUM (50% power) for 18 to 20 minutes. Place baking dish on a wire rack and let set for 5 minutes. Divide into 8 servings.

Each serving equals:

HE: 2½ Protein • 1½ Vegetable • 1 Bread

234 Calories • 6 gm Fat • 24 gm Protein •
21 gm Carbohydrate • 943 mg Sodium • 2 gm Fiber

DIABETIC: 2½ Meat • 1 Vegetable • 1 Starch

Grandma's Modern Meat Loaf

If my grandma were still cooking up a storm today, I know she'd have a meat loaf recipe just like this one. It tastes deliciously old-fashioned and cooks up so rich with flavor, you won't have to an-nounce that dinner is served—everyone will already be seated at the table, forks at the ready!   ❍ Serves 6

> 16 ounces ground 90% lean turkey or beef
> 6 tablespoons (1½ ounces) dried fine bread crumbs
> 1 cup chopped onion
> 1 cup (one 8-ounce can) Hunt's Tomato Sauce☆
> 1 tablespoon Brown Sugar Twin
> 2 teaspoons prepared mustard
> 1 teaspoon dried parsley flakes
> ¼ teaspoon black pepper

In a large bowl, combine meat, bread crumbs, onion, ⅓ cup tomato sauce, Brown Sugar Twin, mustard, parsley flakes, and black pepper. Mix well to combine. Place a small custard cup in center of a deep-dish 9-inch glass pie plate or use a microwave ring mold. Evenly spread meat mixture into plate. Spoon remaining ⅔ cup tomato sauce evenly over top. Microwave on HIGH (100% power) for 8 minutes. Turn pie plate and continue microwaving on HIGH for 8 minutes. Place pie plate on a wire rack and let set for 5 minutes. Cut into 6 servings.

Each serving equals:

> HE: 2 Protein • 1 Vegetable • ½ Bread •
> 1 Optional Calorie
> _____
> 163 Calories • 7 gm Fat • 15 gm Protein •
> 10 gm Carbohydrate • 415 mg Sodium • 1 gm Fiber
> _____
> DIABETIC: 2 Meat • 1 Vegetable • ½ Starch

Stuffed Green Peppers

Here's a midwestern classic no quick cook should be without! The toughest part (well, not really . . .) is picking six perfect peppers to fill with this mix of tasty meat, rice, and spices. The cheese is part of a new tradition—and makes a really good dish GREAT!

● Serves 6

> 6 medium-sized green bell peppers
> 8 ounces ground 90% lean turkey or beef
> ½ cup chopped onion
> 1 cup hot cooked rice
> ½ teaspoon dried minced garlic
> 1 teaspoon Italian seasoning
> 1¾ cups (one 15-ounce can) Hunt's Chunky Tomato Sauce☆
> ¾ cup (3 ounces) shredded Kraft reduced-fat mozzarella cheese

Cut a thin slice from stem end of each green pepper. Remove seeds and membrane. Rinse peppers. Place peppers cut side up in a 9-by-13-inch baking dish. Cover and vent one corner. Microwave on HIGH (100% power) for 3 minutes. Remove from microwave. In a large bowl, combine uncooked meat, onion, rice, garlic, Italian seasoning, and 1 cup tomato sauce. Stuff each pepper with about ½ cup meat mixture. Pour remaining ¾ cup tomato sauce evenly over tops of peppers. Re-cover and vent one corner. Continue microwaving on HIGH for 12 minutes, turning dish every 4 minutes. Sprinkle mozzarella cheese evenly over top and continue microwaving on HIGH, uncovered, for 30 to 45 seconds or until cheese starts to melt. Place baking dish on a wire rack and let set for 5 minutes.

HINT: ⅔ cup uncooked rice usually cooks to about 1 cup.

Each serving equals:

HE: 2⅓ Vegetable • 1⅔ Protein • ⅓ Bread

157 Calories • 5 gm Fat • 13 gm Protein •
15 gm Carbohydrate • 651 mg Sodium • 2 gm Fiber

DIABETIC: 2 Vegetable • 1½ Meat • ½ Starch

Great Northern Bean Bonanza

Can you imagine it—a hearty baked beans dish prepared in minutes in the microwave?! Great flavor, healthy ingredients, and so light on calories you'll want to serve it with everything!

● Serves 4 (full ½ cup)

> ½ cup water
>
> 10 ounces (one 16-ounce can) great northern beans, rinsed and drained
>
> ½ cup chopped onion
>
> 2 teaspoons prepared mustard
>
> ¼ cup Heinz Light Harvest or Healthy Choice ketchup
>
> ½ cup (3 ounces) diced Dubuque 97% fat-free ham or any extra-lean ham
>
> ½ teaspoon prepared horseradish
>
> 2 tablespoons Brown Sugar Twin
>
> ¼ teaspoon black pepper

In an 8-cup glass measuring bowl, combine water and great northern beans. Add onion, mustard, ketchup, ham, horseradish, Brown Sugar Twin, and black pepper. Mix well to combine. Cover and microwave on MEDIUM (60% power) for 15 minutes, turning bowl after every 5 minutes. Place bowl on a wire rack and let set for 5 minutes. Mix well before serving.

Each serving equals:

HE: 1¾ Protein • ¼ Vegetable • 17 Optional Calories

---

137 Calories • 1 gm Fat • 10 gm Protein •
22 gm Carbohydrate • 218 mg Sodium • 5 gm Fiber

DIABETIC: 1½ Starch • 1 Meat

Glazed Carrots with Ham and Apples

The colors of this dish are so pretty, it makes a wonderful accompaniment to any festive meal during the holidays or as the leaves are changing. Sweet and tangy, crisp and a little tart, this recipe celebrates the wonders of the harvest.   ● Serves 4 (1 cup)

3 cups sliced carrots

2 tablespoons water

1½ cups (3 small) peeled, chopped tart cooking apples

1 full cup (6 ounces) diced Dubuque 97% fat-free ham or any extra-lean ham

¼ cup Cary's Sugar Free Maple Syrup

In an 8-cup glass measuring bowl, combine carrots and water. Cover and microwave on HIGH (100% power) for 5 minutes. Stir in apples, ham, and maple syrup. Re-cover and continue microwaving on HIGH for 5 minutes. Mix well before serving.

Each serving equals:

HE: 1½ Vegetable • 1 Protein • ¾ Fruit •
10 Optional Calories

114 Calories • 2 gm Fat • 7 gm Protein •
17 gm Carbohydrate • 409 mg Sodium • 3 gm Fiber

DIABETIC: 1½ Vegetable • 1 Protein • 1 Fruit

Maple Apple Raisin Custard

Don't apples and raisins seem to have a special flavor friendship? At the heart of this creamy custard is their special sweetness, made more delicately delicious with the addition of the maple syrup.

○ Serves 4

> 1 (4-serving) package JELL-O sugar-free vanilla cook-and-serve pudding mix
> ⅔ cup Carnation Nonfat Dry Milk Powder
> 1 cup water
> ½ cup Cary's Sugar Free Maple Syrup
> 1 cup (2 small) diced cooking apples
> ¼ cup raisins

In an 8-cup glass measuring bowl, combine dry pudding mix and dry milk powder. Add water and maple syrup. Mix well using a wire whisk. Stir in apples and raisins. Cover and microwave on HIGH (100% power) for 4 minutes, stirring after every minute. Evenly spoon mixture into 4 dessert dishes. Serve at once.

HINT: Also good served cold with 1 tablespoon Cool Whip Lite, but don't forget to count the few additional calories.

Each serving equals:

HE: 1 Fruit • ¼ Skim Milk • ½ Slider •
8 Optional Calories

---

120 Calories • 0 gm Fat • 4 gm Protein •
26 gm Carbohydrate • 217 mg Sodium • 1 gm Fiber

DIABETIC: 1 Starch *or* Carbohydrate • 1 Fruit

Cinnamon Raisin Nut Pudding

I love a pudding with crunch—just for the surprising change in texture! This smooth and luscious taste treat leaves you feeling so cozy warm and satisfied. The raisins do especially well in the microwave, which plumps them up and makes them taste even sweeter! ● Serves 4 (½ cup)

1 (4-serving) package JELL-O sugar-free vanilla cook-and-serve
    pudding mix
1 teaspoon ground cinnamon
⅔ cup Carnation Nonfat Dry Milk Powder
1½ cups water
1 teaspoon vanilla extract
¼ cup (1 ounce) chopped walnuts
½ cup raisins
¼ cup Cool Whip Lite

In an 8-cup glass measuring bowl, combine dry pudding mix, cinnamon, dry milk powder, and water. Mix well using a wire whisk. Cover and microwave on HIGH (100% power) for 4 minutes, stirring after every minute. Stir in vanilla extract, walnuts, and raisins. Evenly spoon mixture into 4 dessert dishes. Refrigerate for at least 30 minutes. When serving, top each with 1 tablespoon Cool Whip Lite and, if desired, lightly sprinkle with additional cinnamon.

Each serving equals:

HE: 1 Fruit • ½ Skim Milk • ½ Fat • ¼ Protein •
¼ Slider • 8 Optional Calories

177 Calories • 5 gm Fat • 5 gm Protein •
28 gm Carbohydrate • 180 mg Sodium • 1 gm Fiber

DIABETIC: 1 Fruit • 1 Skim Milk • 1 Fat *or*
1 Fruit • 1 Carbohydrate • 1 Fat

Comfort Rice and Raisin Pudding

Rice pudding is one of my favorite childhood memories, and I've created dozens of recipes celebrating the wonders of this lovely, smooth dessert. It's ready so quickly when prepared in the microwave, too! ☉ Serves 8

> 2 (4-serving) packages JELL-O sugar-free vanilla cook-and-serve
>   pudding mix
> 4 cups skim milk
> 1 cup raisins
> 1⅓ cups (4 ounces) uncooked instant rice
> 1 teaspoon vanilla extract

In an 8-cup glass measuring bowl, combine dry pudding mix and skim milk. Add raisins and uncooked rice. Mix well to combine. Cover and microwave on HIGH (100% power) for 6 to 7 minutes, stirring every 2 minutes. Add vanilla extract. Mix gently to combine. Place bowl on a wire rack and let set for 2 to 3 minutes. Evenly spoon mixture into 8 dessert dishes. Serve warm or cold.

Each serving equals:

HE: 1 Fruit • ½ Skim Milk • ½ Bread • ¼ Slider

136 Calories • 0 gm Fat • 7 gm Protein •
27 gm Carbohydrate • 120 mg Sodium • 1 gm Fiber

DIABETIC: 1 Fruit • ½ Skim Milk • ½ Starch

Banana Rhubarb Tapioca Pudding

Cliff loves tapioca, so I'm always looking for delicious new ways to please his truck drivin' man's taste buds! Rhubarb all by itself is a good-enough reason to celebrate the arrival of spring, and this particular pudding looks as heavenly as it tastes!

● Serves 4

> ¾ cup water
> ¼ cup Sugar Twin or Sprinkle Sweet
> 1 (4-serving) package JELL-O sugar-free strawberry gelatin
> 3 tablespoons quick-cooking Minute tapioca
> 3 cups chopped rhubarb
> 1 cup (1 medium) diced banana

In an 8-cup glass measuring bowl, combine water, Sugar Twin, dry gelatin, and tapioca. Let set for 5 minutes. Stir in rhubarb and banana. Cover and microwave on HIGH (100% power) for 7 to 10 minutes or until rhubarb is tender, stirring after 4 minutes. Place bowl on a wire rack and let set for 5 minutes. Evenly spoon into 4 dessert dishes. Good warm or cold.

Each serving equals:

HE: 1½ Vegetable • ½ Fruit • ½ Slider •
3 Optional Calories

---

92 Calories • 0 gm Fat • 2 gm Protein •
21 gm Carbohydrate • 61 mg Sodium • 2 gm Fiber

DIABETIC: ½ Starch • ½ Fruit • 1 Free Food *or*
1 Carbohydrate

Peach Harvest Pie

Ripe peaches may be one of the three or four most scrumptious foods on earth! When the harvest is at its height, why not tempt the ones you love with a luscious, crunchy-sweet pie that just can't be under 200 calories per serving—can it? ● Serves 8

> 1 (4-serving) package JELL-O sugar-free instant vanilla pudding mix
> 2 tablespoons Brown Sugar Twin
> ½ cup (1½ ounces) Kellogg's low-fat Granola cereal
> 3 cups (6 medium) peeled, sliced fresh peaches
> 1 (6-ounce) Keebler graham cracker piecrust

In an 8-cup glass measuring bowl, combine dry pudding mix, Brown Sugar Twin, and Granola cereal. Add sliced peaches. Mix well to combine. Cover and microwave on HIGH (100% power) for 10 to 12 minutes or until peaches are soft and mixture thickens, stirring after every 3 minutes. Pour hot mixture into piecrust. Refrigerate for at least 2 hours. Cut into 8 servings.

HINT: Good served with 1 tablespoon Cool Whip Lite, but don't forget to count the few additional calories.

Each serving equals:

HE: ¾ Bread • ¾ Fruit • ¾ Slider • 4 Optional Calories

174 Calories • 6 gm Fat • 2 gm Protein •
28 gm Carbohydrate • 304 mg Sodium • 2 gm Fiber

DIABETIC: 1 Starch • 1 Fruit • 1 Fat *or*
2 Carbohydrate • 1 Fat

Easy Baked Apple Treats

An apple a day—well, we all know what they say about apples and staying healthy, don't we? But when you slice the apples, drench them in maple syrup, and add a few pecans, you create a taste treat that'll inspire anyone who tastes it to live healthy for a lifetime!

● Serves 4 (½ cup)

> 2 cups (4 small) cored, peeled, and sliced baking apples
>
> ¼ cup Cary's Sugar Free Maple Syrup
>
> 1 tablespoon (¼ ounce) chopped pecans

Arrange apple slices in an 8-by-8-inch glass microwavable baking dish. Drizzle maple syrup over apples. Evenly sprinkle pecans over top. Cover and microwave on HIGH (100% power) for 3 to 4 minutes. Serve warm.

Each serving equals:

HE: 1 Fruit • ¼ Fat • 10 Optional Calories

53 Calories • 1 gm Fat • 0 gm Protein •
11 gm Carbohydrate • 20 mg Sodium • 1 gm Fiber

DIABETIC: 1 Fruit

From the Stove Top

O ne of the reasons I enjoy cooking on the top of the stove is that there is no mystery about it. Instead of having to peek through the oven or microwave door to check on your food, instead of listening to your slow cooker bubble along and wondering "how it's doing," skillet cooking happens right there in front of you. You control the heat, you stir the pot, and you get to enjoy the scrumptious aroma of the dish you're preparing right under your nose!

Here's a secret for easy stove-top preparation (though I recommend this step for all my recipes): Have every ingredient checked, ready, and close at hand—vegetables chopped, cheese measured out, and spices all ready to be added when the recipe calls for them. If you haven't got much counter space near your stove, experiment with setting a cookie sheet over two unused burners and placing your ingredients right next to where you're working. But make certain it won't tip over easily.

You'll find that cleanup is especially simple as long as you coat your skillet with cooking spray before you begin.

As one pot meals go, these dishes are among the quickest and tastiest. Even if you don't think you're much of a cook, you'll feel like a chef as you set those ingredients to sizzling in your pan!

From the Stove Top

From the Stove Top (*continued*)

Mexican Vegetable Beef Soup

A hearty soup that's rich enough to make a meal of is a wonderful addition to your cold-weather repertoire! Because it blends the best of frozen and canned vegetables, you can make this tangy soup-stew any time of the year.   ● Serves 6 (1½ cups)

  8 ounces ground 90% lean turkey or beef
  1 cup chopped onion
  2 cups (one 16-ounce can) tomatoes, coarsely chopped and
      undrained
  1¾ cups (one 15-ounce can) Swanson Beef Broth
  1¾ cups (one 15-ounce can) Hunt's Chunky Tomato Sauce
  1½ cups diced celery
  1½ cups frozen sliced carrots
  1½ cups frozen cut green beans
  2 teaspoons chili seasoning mix
  ¾ cup frozen whole kernel corn
  6 ounces (one 8-ounce can) red kidney beans, rinsed and drained
  1 teaspoon dried parsley flakes

In a large saucepan sprayed with butter-flavored cooking spray, brown meat and onion. Stir in undrained tomatoes, beef broth, and tomato sauce. Bring mixture to a boil. Add celery, carrots, green beans, chili seasoning mix, corn, kidney beans, and parsley flakes. Mix well to combine. Lower heat, cover and simmer for 30 minutes, or until vegetables are tender.

Each serving equals:

HE: 3 Vegetable • 1½ Protein • ½ Bread •
6 Optional Calories

180 Calories • 4 gm Fat • 13 gm Protein •
23 gm Carbohydrate • 817 mg Sodium • 6 gm Fiber

DIABETIC: 2½ Vegetable • 1½ Meat • 1 Starch *or*
2 Carbohydrate • 1 Meat

Italian Zucchini and Spaghetti

Here's my vote for a perfect end-of-summer culinary celebration, just right for when the zucchini are abundant! (You'll notice I leave the peel on so you can enjoy the benefits of extra fiber.) Can you imagine having such a flavorful meal that's ready in about fifteen minutes? ☻ Serves 4 (1 cup)

> 2 cups unpeeled diced zucchini
> ½ cup diced onion
> 1¾ cups (one 15-ounce can) Hunt's Chunky Tomato Sauce
> ¼ cup water
> ¼ cup (¾ ounce) grated Kraft fat-free Parmesan cheese
> ¼ teaspoon dried minced garlic
> 1 teaspoon Italian seasoning
> 1 teaspoon Sugar Twin or Sprinkle Sweet
> 2 cups hot cooked spaghetti, rinsed and drained

In a large skillet sprayed with olive oil–flavored cooking spray, sauté zucchini and onion for 5 minutes or until tender. Add tomato sauce, water, Parmesan cheese, garlic, Italian seasoning, and Sugar Twin. Mix well to combine. Stir in spaghetti. Lower heat and simmer for 10 minutes, stirring occasionally.

HINT: 1½ cups uncooked spaghetti usually cooks to about 2 cups.

Each serving equals:

HE: 3 Vegetable • 1 Bread • ¼ Protein •
1 Optional Calorie

---

156 Calories • 0 gm Fat • 8 gm Protein •
31 gm Carbohydrate • 773 mg Sodium • 3 gm Fiber

DIABETIC: 3 Vegetable • 1 Starch • ½ Meat *or*
2 Carbohydrate • ½ Meat

El Grande Garden Vegetable Skillet

Tumble all these colorful veggies together in one sizzling pan, add the spicy salsa of your choice, and you've got a fantastic summer supper! Why not make a point of serving at least one meatless entree each week, and start with this one?

● Serves 4 (1¼ cups)

> 1 cup coarsely chopped onion
> 1 cup coarsely chopped green bell pepper
> 3 full cups (16 ounces) diced cooked potatoes
> 1½ cups chopped fresh tomatoes
> ½ cup chunky salsa (mild, medium, or hot)
> 1 teaspoon chili seasoning
> ½ teaspoon dried minced garlic
> 1 teaspoon dried parsley flakes
> ¼ teaspoon black pepper

In a large skillet sprayed with olive oil–flavored cooking spray, sauté onion, green pepper, and potatoes for 5 minutes, stirring often. Stir in tomatoes, salsa, chili seasoning, garlic, parsley flakes, and black pepper. Continue cooking for 5 minutes or until mixture is heated through, stirring occasionally.

Each serving equals:

HE: 2 Vegetable • 1 Bread

152 Calories • 0 gm Fat • 4 gm Protein •
34 gm Carbohydrate • 127 mg Sodium • 4 gm Fiber

DIABETIC: 1½ Starch • 1 Vegetable

Green Beans Marinara Spaghetti

For this ten-minute triumph, I simply stirred Cliff's most favorite vegetable (green beans) into a traditional spaghetti dish with marinara sauce. Topped with cheese, spiced with bits of basil and oregano, this one will quickly become a family favorite!

● Serves 4 (1 cup)

> ½ cup chopped onion
>
> 1¾ cups (one 15-ounce can) Hunt's Chunky Tomato Sauce
>
> ½ teaspoon dried minced garlic
>
> 2 teaspoons Italian seasoning
>
> 2 cups (one 16-ounce can) cut green beans, rinsed and drained
>
> 2 cups hot cooked spaghetti, rinsed and drained
>
> ¼ cup (¾ ounce) grated Kraft fat-free Parmesan cheese

In a large skillet sprayed with olive oil–flavored cooking spray, sauté onion for 5 minutes or until tender. Add tomato sauce. Mix well to combine. Stir in garlic, Italian seasoning, green beans, and spaghetti. Lower heat and simmer for 5 minutes, stirring occasionally. Stir in Parmesan cheese. Serve at once.

HINT: 1½ cups uncooked spaghetti usually cooks to about 2 cups.

Each serving equals:

HE: 4 Vegetable • 1 Bread • ¼ Protein

160 Calories • 0 gm Fat • 8 gm Protein •
32 gm Carbohydrate • 772 mg Sodium • 3 gm Fiber

DIABETIC: 3 Vegetable • 1 Starch • ½ Meat

Linguine and Tuna Skillet

This is almost a tuna "alfredo," it's so creamy and luscious—and good for making sure you're getting your calcium, too! Peas make a colorful and tasty addition to this quick-and-easy "pleasure in a pan"!   ❂   Serves 4 (1 cup)

1½ cups (one 12-fluid-ounce can) Carnation Evaporated Skim
    Milk
3 tablespoons all-purpose flour
¼ teaspoon black pepper
1 teaspoon dried onion flakes
1 teaspoon dried parsley flakes
½ cup frozen peas
1 (6-ounce) can white tuna, packed in water, drained and flaked
¼ cup (¾ ounce) grated Kraft fat-free Parmesan cheese
2 cups cooked linguine, rinsed and drained

In a covered jar, combine evaporated skim milk and flour. Shake well to blend. Pour milk mixture into a large skillet sprayed with butter-flavored cooking spray. Add black pepper, onion flakes, parsley flakes, and peas. Mix well to combine. Cook over medium heat, stirring often, until mixture thickens. Stir in tuna, Parmesan cheese, and linguine. Lower heat and simmer for 5 minutes, or until mixture is heated through, stirring often.

HINTS: 1.   1½ cups uncooked broken linguine usually cooks to about 2 cups.

         2.   Spaghetti or noodles may be substituted for linguine.

Each serving equals:

HE: 1½ Bread • 1 Protein • ¾ Skim Milk

275 Calories • 2 gm Fat • 25 gm Protein •
39 gm Carbohydrate • 360 mg Sodium • 3 gm Fiber

DIABETIC: 2 Meat • 1½ Starch • 1 Skim Milk

New Orleans Fish Creole Hash

Creole food traditions promise fragrant, flavorful dishes, and this one is no exception! A hash combo is a good way to get your family to eat more fish—and enjoy its health benefits too. Don't forget to include the Worcestershire sauce's uniquely tangy taste!

● Serves 4 (1¼ cups)

> 16 ounces white fish, cut into 16 pieces
> ½ cup chopped onion
> ½ cup chopped celery
> ½ cup chopped green bell pepper
> 1¾ cups (one 15-ounce can) Hunt's Chunky Tomato Sauce
> ½ teaspoon dried minced garlic
> 1 teaspoon Worcestershire sauce
> 2 cups hot cooked rice

In a large skillet sprayed with butter-flavored cooking spray, sauté fish pieces, onion, celery, and green pepper for 8 to 10 minutes or until vegetables are tender. Stir in tomato sauce, garlic, and Worcestershire sauce. Add rice. Mix well to combine. Lower heat, cover and simmer for 15 minutes, stirring occasionally.

HINT: 1⅓ cups uncooked rice usually cooks to about 2 cups.

Each serving equals:

HE: 2½ Vegetable • 1½ Protein • 1 Bread

---

246 Calories • 2 gm Fat • 25 gm Protein •
32 gm Carbohydrate • 406 mg Sodium • 3 gm Fiber

DIABETIC: 3 Meat • 1½ Starch • 1 Vegetable *or*
3 Meat • 2 Carbohydrate

Tomato-Chicken-Rice Soup

If you love chicken soup but you're looking for something new and fun, here's a hearty tomato soup so rich with chicken and rice it's practically a stew! The rosy color of the broth, and the sweetness the tomato sauce adds, make this a memorable beginning to any meal.   ☻   Serves 4 (1½ cups)

> 1 full cup (6 ounces) diced cooked chicken breast
> 2 cups (one 16-ounce can) Healthy Request Chicken Broth
> 1 cup water
> 1¾ cups (one 15-ounce can) Hunt's Chunky Tomato Sauce
> 1⅓ cups (4 ounces) uncooked instant rice
> 1 teaspoon dried parsley flakes
> 1 teaspoon dried onion flakes
> ¼ teaspoon black pepper
> 2 teaspoons Sugar Twin or Sprinkle Sweet

In a large saucepan, combine chicken breast, chicken broth, water, and tomato sauce. Bring mixture to a boil. Stir in rice, parsley flakes, onion flakes, black pepper, and Sugar Twin. Lower heat, cover, and simmer for 15 minutes, or until rice is tender, stirring occasionally.

HINT: If you don't have leftovers, purchase a chunk of cooked chicken breast from your local deli.

Each serving equals:

HE: 1¾ Vegetable • 1½ Protein • 1 Bread • 16 Optional Calories

158 Calories • 2 gm Fat • 17 gm Protein • 18 gm Carbohydrate • 974 mg Sodium • 0 gm Fiber

DIABETIC: 1½ Meat • 1 Vegetable • 1 Starch

Home-Style Chicken and Cabbage Stew

Here's a traditional, old-world-style cabbage dish brought deliciously up to date! The soy sauce may seem like a surprise, but it's my little secret to bringing out the special flavors of this satisfying dish.   ● Serves 4 (1 full cup)

> 2 cups (one 16-ounce can) Healthy Request Chicken Broth☆
>
> 1 full cup (3 ounces) uncooked broken vermicelli noodles
>
> 1 cup shredded carrots
>
> 2 cups shredded cabbage
>
> ½ cup chopped onion
>
> 1 full cup (6 ounces) diced cooked chicken breast
>
> ½ cup (one 2.5-ounce jar) sliced mushrooms, drained
>
> 2 tablespoons reduced-sodium soy sauce

Reserve ¼ cup chicken broth. In a medium saucepan, cook noodles in remaining 1¾ cups chicken broth for 8 minutes or until tender. Meanwhile, pour reserved chicken broth into a large skillet sprayed with butter-flavored cooking spray. Add carrots, cabbage, and onion. Mix well to combine. Cook over medium heat for 8 minutes or until vegetables are tender, stirring often. Stir in undrained noodles, chicken, mushrooms, and soy sauce. Lower heat and simmer for 10 minutes, stirring occasionally.

HINTS: 1. If you can't find vermicelli noodles, use spaghetti.

2. If you don't have leftovers, purchase a chunk of cooked chicken breast from your local deli.

Each serving equals:

HE: 2 Vegetable • 1½ Protein • 1 Bread •
8 Optional Calories

162 Calories • 2 gm Fat • 18 gm Protein •
18 gm Carbohydrate • 391 mg Sodium • 3 gm Fiber

DIABETIC: 2 Vegetable • 1½ Meat • 1 Starch

Chicken Green Bean Skillet

You can practically taste spoonfuls of cream in this smooth-as-silk chicken skillet—but you know even before you finish it that your taste buds have been fooled! The skim milk and creamy soup make culinary magic together.   ☉   Serves 4

½ cup chopped onion

1 full cup (6 ounces) diced cooked chicken breast

4 cups (two 16-ounce cans) French-style green beans, rinsed and drained

1 (10¾-ounce) can Healthy Request Cream of Chicken Soup

2 tablespoons skim milk

¼ teaspoon black pepper

In a large skillet sprayed with butter-flavored cooking spray, sauté onion and chicken for 5 minutes or until onion is tender. Add green beans, chicken soup, skim milk, and black pepper. Mix well to combine. Lower heat and simmer for 5 minutes or until mixture is heated through, stirring often.

HINTS: 1. If you don't have leftovers, purchase a chunk of cooked chicken breast from your local deli.

2. Good as is or served over rice, pasta, or potatoes.

Each serving equals:

HE: 2¼ Vegetable • 1½ Protein • ½ Slider •
10 Optional Calories

159 Calories • 3 gm Fat • 17 gm Protein •
16 gm Carbohydrate • 370 mg Sodium • 2 gm Fiber

DIABETIC: 2 Vegetable • 1½ Meat • ½ Starch

Indian Rice with Chicken

If you're unfamiliar with Indian cooking, you may look with some confusion at the ingredients in this unusual dish from halfway around the world. But Indian cuisine makes a delicious habit of blending textures and tastes in fresh ways, so that this blend of spices with nuts, raisins, and rice will delight all who try it!

● Serves 6 (scant 1 cup)

> 2 cups (one 16-ounce can) Healthy Request Chicken Broth
>
> 1 teaspoon curry powder
>
> 1 teaspoon dried parsley flakes
>
> 1/4 teaspoon ground ginger
>
> 1 1/2 cups (8 ounces) diced cooked chicken breast
>
> 1/4 cup (1 ounce) chopped dry-roasted peanuts
>
> 3/4 cup raisins
>
> 2 cups (6 ounces) uncooked instant rice

In a large skillet, combine chicken broth, curry powder, parsley flakes, and ginger. Stir in chicken, peanuts, and raisins. Bring mixture to a boil. Add rice. Mix well to combine. Remove from heat. Cover and let set 5 minutes. Stir again before serving.

HINT: If you don't have leftovers, purchase a chunk of cooked chicken breast from your local deli.

Each serving equals:

HE: 1 1/2 Protein • 1 Bread • 1 Fruit • 1/3 Fat •
5 Optional Calories

212 Calories • 4 gm Fat • 16 gm Protein •
28 gm Carbohydrate • 192 mg Sodium • 1 gm Fiber

DIABETIC: 1 1/2 Meat • 1 Starch • 1 Fruit

Caribbean Chicken

Here's another kitchen culture that enjoys unexpected combinations. This island entree turns a mélange of fruits, vegetables, and spices into a dish fit to serve in paradise!

○ Serves 6 (1 cup)

16 ounces skinned and boned uncooked chicken breast, cut into 36 pieces
2 cups (two 8-ounce cans) pineapple chunks, packed in fruit juice, drained, and ¼ cup liquid reserved
1 cup chopped green bell pepper
1 cup water
1 tablespoon cornstarch
2 tablespoons cider vinegar
2 tablespoons Brown Sugar Twin
¼ teaspoon dried minced garlic
1 cup (1 medium) diced banana
⅓ cup (1½ ounce) chopped cashews

In a large skillet sprayed with butter-flavored cooking spray, sauté chicken for 5 minutes or until tender. Stir in pineapple and green pepper. In a covered jar, combine reserved pineapple liquid, water, cornstarch, vinegar, Brown Sugar Twin, and garlic. Shake well to blend. Pour mixture into chicken mixture. Mix well to combine. Continue cooking for 5 minutes or until mixture thickens, stirring often. Fold in banana and cashews. Lower heat and simmer for 3 to 4 minutes.

HINT: Good served as is or spooned over rice.

Each serving equals:

HE: 2¼ Protein • 1 Fruit • ½ Fat • ⅓ Vegetable • 7 Optional Calories

208 Calories • 4 gm Fat • 19 gm Protein • 24 gm Carbohydrate • 96 mg Sodium • 1 gm Fiber

DIABETIC: 2 Meat • 1 Fruit • ½ Fat

Continental Alfredo Skillet

This delightfully different entree takes some of the ingredients featured in dishes like chicken cordon bleu and transforms them into a party that deserves the name "alfredo," that most luscious of all creamy pastas! The lemon pepper is one of my best kitchen secrets.

● Serves 4 (1 cup)

> 1½ cups (one 12-fluid-ounce can) Carnation Evaporated Skim Milk
>
> 3 tablespoons all-purpose flour
>
> ¼ teaspoon lemon pepper
>
> ¼ cup (¾ ounce) grated Kraft fat-free Parmesan cheese
>
> 4 cups (two 16-ounce cans) cut green beans, rinsed and drained
>
> 1 cup (5 ounces) diced cooked chicken breast
>
> 1 full cup (6 ounces) diced Dubuque 97% fat-free ham or any extra-lean ham

In a covered jar, combine evaporated skim milk and flour. Shake well to blend. Pour mixture into a large saucepan sprayed with butter-flavored cooking spray. Add lemon pepper and Parmesan cheese. Mix well to combine. Cook over medium heat, stirring often, until mixture thickens. Add green beans, chicken, and ham. Mix well to combine. Lower heat and simmer for 5 minutes or until mixture is heated through, stirring often.

HINT: If you don't have leftovers, purchase a chunk of cooked chicken breast from your local deli.

Each serving equals:

HE: 2¼ Protein • 2 Vegetable • ¾ Skim Milk • ¼ Bread • ¼ Protein

239 Calories • 3 gm Fat • 29 gm Protein • 24 gm Carbohydrate • 568 mg Sodium • 2 gm Fiber

DIABETIC: 2 Meat • 2 Vegetable • ½ Skim Milk • ½ Starch

Turkey Macaroni Dinner

Here's a great way to re-invent leftover turkey that will be especially welcome during the holidays! You'll be amazed how a bit of flour and some milk powder join hands to create an unforgettably good gravy! ☺ Serves 6 (1 cup)

2 cups (one 16-ounce can) Healthy Request Chicken Broth

3 tablespoons all-purpose flour

⅔ cup Carnation Nonfat Dry Milk Powder

2 teaspoons dried parsley flakes

⅛ teaspoon black pepper

½ teaspoon poultry seasoning

2 cups hot cooked elbow macaroni, rinsed and drained

½ cup frozen whole kernel corn

2 full cups (12 ounces) diced cooked turkey breast

In a covered jar, combine chicken broth, flour, and dry milk powder. Shake well to blend. Pour mixture into a large skillet sprayed with butter-flavored cooking spray. Add parsley flakes, black pepper, and poultry seasoning. Mix well to combine. Cook over medium heat, stirring often, until mixture thickens and starts to boil. Stir in macaroni, corn, and turkey. Lower heat and simmer for 10 minutes or until mixture is heated through, stirring occasionally.

HINTS: 1. 1⅓ cups uncooked macaroni usually cooks to about 2 cups.

2. If you don't have leftovers, purchase a chunk of cooked turkey breast from your local deli.

Each serving equals:

HE: 2 Protein • 1 Bread • ⅓ Skim Milk • 5 Optional Calories

206 Calories • 2 gm Fat • 24 gm Protein • 23 gm Carbohydrate • 245 mg Sodium • 1 gm Fiber

DIABETIC: 2 Meat • 1½ Starch

Hamburger Milk Gravy Hash

My son Tommy loves anything with the name "hamburger milk gravy," so this hash was created to make him smile! It's so thick with meat and potatoes, it's been a winner with every man who's ever tried it. With that recommendation, I hope you'll put it on your "to try" list very soon! ☻ Serves 4 (1 cup)

> 8 ounces ground 90% lean turkey or beef
> ½ cup chopped onion
> ½ teaspoon dried minced garlic
> 2½ cups (12 ounces) chopped cooked potatoes
> ½ cup (one 2.5-ounce jar) sliced mushrooms, drained
> 1½ cups (one 12-fluid-ounce can) Carnation Evaporated Skim Milk
> 3 tablespoons all-purpose flour
> 1 tablespoon dried parsley flakes

In a large skillet sprayed with butter-flavored cooking spray, brown meat, onion, and garlic. Add potatoes and mushrooms. Mix well to combine. Continue cooking for 5 minutes or until potatoes are browned, stirring occasionally. In a covered jar, combine evaporated skim milk and flour. Shake well to blend. Add milk mixture to meat mixture. Mix well to combine. Stir in parsley flakes. Lower heat and simmer for 5 minutes or until mixture thickens, stirring occasionally.

Each serving equals:

HE: 1½ Protein • 1 Bread • ¾ Skim Milk • ½ Vegetable

253 Calories • 5 gm Fat • 20 gm Protein •
32 gm Carbohydrate • 254 mg Sodium • 1 gm Fiber

DIABETIC: 1½ Meat • 1 Starch • 1 Skim Milk

German Skillet Stew

Sauerkraut is just too delicious to be reserved only for the top of hot dogs, so I often work out ways to include it in my suppers and stews. The caraway seeds give it a tanginess that's very special.

● Serves 4 (1 full cup)

> 8 ounces ground 90% lean turkey or beef
> ¾ cup chopped onion
> 1¾ cups (one 15-ounce can) Hunt's Chunky Tomato Sauce
> ½ cup water
> 1 tablespoon Brown Sugar Twin
> 1 teaspoon dried parsley flakes
> 1 cup cold cooked rice
> 1¾ cups (one 14½-ounce can) Frank's Bavarian-style
>   sauerkraut, drained

In a large skillet sprayed with butter-flavored cooking spray, brown meat and onion. Stir in tomato sauce, water, Brown Sugar Twin, and parsley flakes. Add rice and sauerkraut. Mix well to combine. Lower heat and simmer for 15 minutes, stirring occasionally.

HINTS: 1.   ⅔ cup uncooked rice usually cooks to about 1 cup.

       2.   If you can't find Bavarian sauerkraut, use regular sauerkraut, ½ teaspoon caraway seeds, and 1 teaspoon Brown Sugar Twin.

Each serving equals:

HE: 3 Vegetable • 1½ Protein • ½ Bread •
1 Optional Calorie

---

189 Calories • 5 gm Fat • 14 gm Protein •
22 gm Carbohydrate • 1239 mg Sodium • 3 gm Fiber

DIABETIC: 2 Vegetable • 1½ Meat • 1 Starch

Cabbage Patch Stew

If you're looking for ways to include more healthy fiber in your daily diet, here's a recipe that delivers lots of it in a truly scrumptious style! Not only that, but you're getting those required daily servings of veggies in one delectable dish! ● Serves 4 (1½ cups)

8 ounces ground 90% lean turkey or beef

½ cup diced onion

1¼ cups diced carrots

2 cups (10 ounces) diced raw potatoes

1¾ cups (one 14½-ounce can) stewed tomatoes, undrained

1 cup (one 8-ounce can) Hunt's Tomato Sauce

⅛ teaspoon black pepper

2 teaspoons dried parsley flakes

1 tablespoon Worcestershire sauce

3 cups coarsely shredded cabbage

In a large skillet sprayed with butter-flavored cooking spray, brown meat and onion. Stir in carrots, potatoes, and undrained stewed tomatoes. Add tomato sauce, black pepper, parsley flakes, and Worcestershire sauce. Mix well to combine. Bring mixture to a boil. Lower heat, cover, and simmer for 15 minutes or until vegetables are just tender. Stir in cabbage. Re-cover and continue simmering for 15 minutes or until cabbage is tender, stirring occasionally.

Each serving equals:

HE: 4¼ Vegetable • 1½ Protein • ½ Bread

213 Calories • 5 gm Fat • 14 gm Protein •
28 gm Carbohydrate • 407 mg Sodium • 4 gm Fiber

DIABETIC: 2 Vegetable • 1½ Meat • 1 Starch

Skillet Supper Dish

If you're on a budget or just trying to cut down your consumption of meat, here's an amazing example of how just a half pound of lean turkey or beef can feed four—but no one will leave the table hungry or disappointed! This is good to try on busy nights, because it can simmer almost unattended while it cooks.

● Serves 4 (1½ cups)

> 8 ounces ground 90% lean turkey or beef
>
> ¼ cup chopped onion
>
> ½ cup (one 2.5-ounce jar) sliced mushrooms, drained
>
> 1 cup shredded carrots
>
> 1½ cups frozen cut green beans
>
> 1¾ cups (one 14½-ounce can) stewed tomatoes, undrained
>
> 1 (10¾-ounce) can Healthy Request Tomato Soup
>
> 1 cup water
>
> 1⅓ cups (3 ounces) uncooked elbow macaroni
>
> ¼ teaspoon black pepper
>
> 1 teaspoon Italian seasoning

In a large skillet sprayed with olive oil–flavored cooking spray, brown meat and onion. Add mushrooms, carrots, green beans, undrained stewed tomatoes, tomato soup, and water. Mix well to combine. Stir in macaroni, black pepper, and Italian seasoning. Lower heat, cover, and simmer for 20 minutes or until macaroni is tender, stirring occasionally.

Each serving equals:

HE: 2½ Vegetable • 1½ Protein • 1 Bread • ½ Slider • 5 Optional Calories

302 Calories • 6 gm Fat • 16 gm Protein • 46 gm Carbohydrate • 710 mg Sodium • 9 gm Fiber

DIABETIC: 2 Vegetable • 2 Starch • 1½ Meat

Mexicali Skillet Dish

I try to "cram" every one of my recipes with lots and lots of flavor, and I think I might be most successful with my Mexican-inspired entrees! This one is speedy, spicy, and oh-so-good!

○ Serves 6 (1 cup)

> 16 ounces ground 90% lean turkey or beef
> ¼ cup chopped onion
> 1¾ cups (one 14½-ounce can) stewed tomatoes, undrained
> ¼ cup water
> 2 teaspoons taco seasoning mix
> ¾ cup frozen peas
> ¾ cup frozen corn
> Scant 1½ cups (2¼ ounces) uncooked noodles

In a large skillet sprayed with olive oil–flavored cooking spray, brown meat and onion. Stir in undrained stewed tomatoes, water, and taco seasoning mix. Add peas, corn, and uncooked noodles. Mix well to combine. Lower heat, cover, and simmer for 10 minutes, or until noodles are tender, stirring occasionally.

Each serving equals:

HE: 2 Protein • 1 Bread • ⅔ Vegetable

219 Calories • 7 gm Fat • 17 gm Protein •
22 gm Carbohydrate • 265 mg Sodium • 3 gm Fiber

DIABETIC: 2 Meat • 1 Starch • ½ Vegetable

"Sausage" and Cabbage Dinner

I didn't set out to "fool" your taste buds, but I think I'll succeed with this sizzling skillet supper. Instead of mixing in high-fat sausage meat, I've mimicked those flavors so believably, your family will be more than convinced you're serving the real thing!

● Serves 4 (1 full cup)

> 8 ounces ground 90% lean turkey or beef
> ½ teaspoon poultry seasoning
> ¼ teaspoon ground sage
> ¼ teaspoon garlic powder
> ½ cup chopped onion
> 3 cups shredded cabbage
> 1 (10¾-ounce) can Healthy Request Cream of Mushroom Soup
> 2 cups cooked noodles, rinsed and drained

In a large skillet sprayed with butter-flavored cooking spray, brown meat. Stir in poultry seasoning, sage, garlic powder, onion, and cabbage. Continue cooking for 5 minutes, or until cabbage is tender and lightly browned, stirring often. Add mushroom soup and noodles. Mix well to combine. Lower heat and simmer for 5 minutes or until mixture is heated through, stirring occasionally.

HINT: 1¾ cups uncooked noodles usually cooks to 2 cups.

Each serving equals:

HE: 1¾ Vegetable • 1½ Protein • 1 Bread • ½ Slider • 1 Optional Calorie

247 Calories • 7 gm Fat • 15 gm Protein • 31 gm Carbohydrate • 385 mg Sodium • 2 gm Fiber

DIABETIC: 1½ Meat • 1½ Starch • 1 Vegetable

Tex-Mex "Sausage" Skillet

Here's another tricky but terrific meal in minutes that delivers the flavor of sausage in a way that's healthier and spicy-good! I invite you to go as hot as you dare with the salsa that gives this recipe its special "zing," but I find it best to go with mild, then provide a jar of spicy stuff for those more "hot to trot!" ❂ Serves 4

8 ounces ground 90% lean turkey or beef

½ teaspoon poultry seasoning

¼ teaspoon ground sage

¼ teaspoon garlic powder

1¾ cups (one 15-ounce can) Hunt's Chunky Tomato Sauce

½ cup chunky salsa (mild, medium, or hot)

1 cup frozen whole kernel corn

⅔ cup (2 ounces) uncooked instant rice

4 (¾-ounce) slices Kraft reduced-fat American cheese, halved diagonally

In a large skillet sprayed with olive oil–flavored cooking spray, brown meat. Stir in poultry seasoning, sage, and garlic powder. Add tomato sauce, salsa, and corn. Mix well to combine. Bring mixture to a boil. Stir in uncooked rice. Evenly arrange cheese triangles over top. Remove from heat, cover, and let set for 5 minutes. Divide into 4 servings.

Each serving equals:

HE: 2½ Protein • 2 Vegetable • 1 Bread

185 Calories • 5 gm Fat • 14 gm Protein •
21 gm Carbohydrate • 946 mg Sodium • 1 gm Fiber

DIABETIC: 2 Meat • 2 Vegetable • 1 Starch

Creamy Spaghetti Skillet

Creamy, cheesy, and full of meaty goodness, this skillet spaghetti dish delivers loads of great taste without loading on the fat! If you're as crazy about mushrooms as some people I know, you may want to add a few more—and if you've got some fresh ones in the fridge, toss 'em in!   ☻ Serves 4 (1 cup)

8 ounces ground 90% lean turkey or beef

½ cup chopped onion

1¾ cups (one 15-ounce can) Hunt's Chunky Tomato Sauce

1½ teaspoons Italian seasoning

1 tablespoon Sugar Twin or Sprinkle Sweet

1 (10¾-ounce) can Healthy Request Cream of Mushroom Soup

½ cup (one 2.5-ounce jar) sliced mushrooms, drained

2 cups hot cooked spaghetti, rinsed and drained

¼ cup (¾ ounce) grated Kraft fat-free Parmesan cheese

In a large skillet sprayed with olive oil–flavored cooking spray, brown meat and onion. Add tomato sauce, Italian seasoning, and Sugar Twin. Mix well to combine. Stir in mushroom soup, mushrooms, spaghetti, and Parmesan cheese. Lower heat and simmer for 10 minutes, stirring occasionally.

HINT: 1½ cups uncooked spaghetti usually cooks to about 2 cups.

Each serving equals:

HE: 2¼ Vegetable • 1¾ Protein • 1 Bread • ½ Slider •
3 Optional Calories

266 Calories • 6 gm Fat • 18 gm Protein •
35 gm Carbohydrate • 1,140 mg Sodium • 2 gm Fiber

DIABETIC: 2 Vegetable • 2 Meat • 1½ Starch

Ranger Beans

Very few recipes could provide this much healthy protein for fewer than 200 calories! Beans are a delicious source of healthy satisfaction and, when blended with just enough lean meat, they'll persuade all your meat lovers that they're getting more than they are!

● Serves 6 (¾ cup)

8 ounces ground 90% lean turkey or beef
½ cup chopped onion
1¾ cups (one 15-ounce can) Hunt's Chunky Tomato Sauce
20 ounces (two 16-ounce cans) great northern beans, rinsed and drained
1 tablespoon Brown Sugar Twin
1 teaspoon chili seasoning mix
¼ teaspoon black pepper

In a large skillet sprayed with butter-flavored cooking spray, brown meat and onion. Stir in tomato sauce. Add great northern beans, Brown Sugar Twin, chili seasoning mix, and black pepper. Mix well to combine. Lower heat and simmer for 10 minutes, stirring occasionally.

Each serving equals:

HE: 2⅔ Protein • 1⅓ Vegetable • 1 Optional Calorie

171 Calories • 3 gm Fat • 15 gm Protein • 21 gm Carbohydrate • 38 mg Sodium • 5 gm Fiber

DIABETIC: 2 Meat • 1 Starch • 1 Vegetable

Grande Noodle Con Carne Skillet

This chili supper is so full of flavor and substance, it deserves to be called "Grande"! The noodles and corn are a little unexpected in a traditional chili, but they make the difference between "pretty darn good" and "doggone fantastic!" ● Serves 4 (1 full cup)

> 8 ounces ground 90% lean turkey or beef
> ¼ cup chopped onion
> 1¾ cups (one 14½-ounce can) stewed tomatoes, coarsely chopped and undrained
> 2 teaspoons chili seasoning mix
> ½ cup frozen whole kernel corn
> 1½ cups cooked noodles

In a large skillet sprayed with olive oil–flavored cooking spray, brown meat and onion. Add undrained stewed tomatoes and chili seasoning mix. Mix well to combine. Stir in corn and noodles. Lower heat and simmer for 10 minutes, stirring occasionally.

HINT: 1¼ cups uncooked noodles usually cooks to about 1½ cups.

Each serving equals:

HE: 1½ Protein • 1 Vegetable • 1 Bread

222 Calories • 6 gm Fat • 15 gm Protein •
27 gm Carbohydrate • 342 mg Sodium • 3 gm Fiber

DIABETIC: 2 Meat • 1 Starch • 1 Vegetable

Cowpoke Hash

You may find yourself humming "Home on the Range" as you prepare this hearty skillet hash! It's just the kind of man-pleasing dish a pack of hungry cowboys might demand on their next roundup—or, at least, for their next tailgate party!

● Serves 4 (1 full cup)

> 1½ cups (8 ounces) diced cooked lean roast beef
>
> ½ cup chopped onion
>
> ½ cup chopped green bell pepper
>
> 1¾ cups (one 15-ounce can) Hunt's Chunky Tomato Sauce
>
> 2 teaspoons chili seasoning mix
>
> 1 tablespoon Brown Sugar Twin
>
> 1½ cups (8 ounces) diced cooked potatoes
>
> 6 ounces (one 8-ounce can) red kidney beans, rinsed and drained

In a large skillet sprayed with olive oil–flavored cooking spray, brown roast beef, onion, and green pepper for 5 minutes or until vegetables are tender. Stir in tomato sauce, chili seasoning mix, and Brown Sugar Twin. Add potatoes and kidney beans. Mix well to combine. Lower heat, cover, and simmer for 10 minutes, stirring occasionally.

Each serving equals:

HE: 2¾ Protein • 2¼ Vegetable • ½ Bread •
1 Optional Calorie

224 Calories • 4 gm Fat • 21 gm Protein •
26 gm Carbohydrate • 741 mg Sodium • 4 gm Fiber

DIABETIC: 2½ Meat • 2 Vegetable • 1 Starch *or*
2½ Meat • 2 Carbohydrate

Farmhouse Pork Stroganoff

It's the richness of sour cream that makes a stroganoff taste sinful! Here's a version that wends its creamy way through an abundance of noodles, made even more delectable by the addition of hearty pork. The veggies add color and flavor to make this so memorable!

⊙ Serves 4 (1 cup)

> 8 ounces ground 90% lean pork
> 1 cup chopped onion
> ½ cup chopped green bell pepper
> ½ cup (one 2.5-ounce jar) sliced mushrooms, drained
> 1 (10¾-ounce) can Healthy Request Tomato Soup
> 1 teaspoon dried parsley flakes
> ¼ teaspoon black pepper
> ¼ cup Land O Lakes no-fat sour cream
> 2 cups cooked noodles, rinsed and drained

In a large skillet sprayed with butter-flavored cooking spray, brown pork, onion, and green pepper for 6 to 8 minutes or until vegetables are tender, stirring often. Add mushrooms, tomato soup, parsley flakes, and black pepper. Mix well to combine. Stir in sour cream and noodles. Lower heat and simmer for 6 to 8 minutes or until mixture is heated through, stirring occasionally.

HINT: 1¾ cups uncooked noodles usually cooks to about 2 cups.

Each serving equals:

HE: 1½ Protein • 1 Bread • 1 Vegetable • ¾ Slider

277 Calories • 5 gm Fat • 19 gm Protein •
39 gm Carbohydrate • 438 mg Sodium • 6 gm Fiber

DIABETIC: 2 Starch • 1½ Meat • 1 Vegetable *or*
2 Carbohydrate • 1½ Meat • 1 Vegetable

Stove-Top Pork Goulash

Here's a dish that tastes just so close to that old-country goodness, you might even fool a Hungarian! If you've never cooked with paprika, its delicate flavor and lush color will win you over after just one bite. Isn't it fun to have so many quick-fix meals that taste simmered, not rushed? ❍ Serves 6 (1 cup)

1½ cups (8 ounces) diced lean cooked roast pork
½ cup chopped onion
1 cup frozen peas
½ cup (one 2.5-ounce jar) sliced mushrooms, drained
1¾ cups (one 15-ounce can) Hunt's Chunky Tomato Sauce
½ teaspoon dried minced garlic
½ teaspoon black pepper
1 teaspoon paprika
¾ cup (3 ounces) shredded Kraft reduced-fat Cheddar cheese
2 cups cooked noodles, rinsed and drained

In a large skillet sprayed with butter-flavored cooking spray, brown pork and onion for 5 minutes, stirring often. Add peas, mushrooms, tomato sauce, garlic, black pepper, and paprika. Mix well to combine. Stir in Cheddar cheese and noodles. Lower heat and simmer for about 5 minutes, stirring occasionally.

HINTS: 1. If you don't have leftovers, purchase a chunk of cooked roast pork from your local deli.

2. 1¾ cups uncooked noodles usually cooks to about 2 cups.

Each serving equals:

HE: 2 Protein • 1½ Vegetable • 1 Bread

209 Calories • 5 gm Fat • 18 gm Protein •
23 gm Carbohydrate • 662 mg Sodium • 3 gm Fiber

DIABETIC: 2 Meat • 1 Vegetable • 1 Starch

Italian Pork Loins

With so many lean cuts of pork now available in our markets, many families are choosing to enjoy this beloved taste more often. This saucy combo is simple but superb, and worth making a regular on your table!   ● Serves 4

> *4 (4-ounce) lean pork tenderloins or cutlets*
> *1¾ cups (one 15-ounce can) Hunt's Chunky Tomato Sauce*
> *½ cup (one 2.5-ounce jar) sliced mushrooms, drained*
> *1 teaspoon Italian seasoning*
> *¼ teaspoon dried minced garlic*
> *2 teaspoons Sugar Twin or Sprinkle Sweet*

In a large skillet sprayed with olive oil–flavored cooking spray, lightly brown pork for 3 minutes on both sides. In a small bowl, combine tomato sauce, mushrooms, Italian seasoning, garlic, and Sugar Twin. Pour sauce mixture evenly over pork. Lower heat, cover, and simmer for 20 minutes. Uncover and continue cooking for 5 minutes. When serving, evenly spoon sauce over pork.

HINT: Don't overbrown meat or it will become tough.

Each serving equals:

HE: 3 Protein • 2 Vegetable • 1 Optional Calorie

---

196 Calories • 6 gm Fat • 28 gm Protein •
7 gm Carbohydrate • 831 mg Sodium • 0 gm Fiber

DIABETIC: 3 Meat • 2 Vegetable

Ham and Green Beans in Mushroom Sauce

Ham is another much-loved food that's too often saved only for special occasions. But when you eat it in moderation as part of a creamy, healthy main dish, you can enjoy it whenever you like. I think you'll be pleased at how tasty lean ham can be!

○ Serves 4 (1 full cup)

1 (10¾-ounce) can Healthy Request Cream of Mushroom Soup
¼ cup skim milk
1 teaspoon dried parsley flakes
1 teaspoon dried onion flakes
⅛ teaspoon black pepper
1 full cup (6 ounces) diced Dubuque 97% fat-free ham or any
    extra-lean ham
4 cups (two 16-ounce cans) cut green beans, rinsed and drained
½ cup (one 2.5-ounce jar) sliced mushrooms, drained

In a large skillet, combine mushroom soup, skim milk, parsley flakes, onion flakes, and black pepper. Cook over medium heat for 2 to 3 minutes, stirring often. Add ham, green beans, and mushrooms. Mix well to combine. Lower heat and simmer for 5 to 7 minutes or until mixture is heated through, stirring occasionally.

Each serving equals:

HE: 2¼ Vegetable • 1 Protein • ½ Slider •
7 Optional Calories

127 Calories • 3 gm Fat • 10 gm Protein •
15 gm Carbohydrate • 770 mg Sodium • 2 gm Fiber

DIABETIC: 2 Vegetable • 1 Meat • ½ Starch *or*
1 Carbohydrate • 1 Meat

Fiesta Ham and Noodle Skillet

This recipe is my idea of a "party on a plate," stirred up in minutes from inexpensive ingredients that ask you to "strike up the band." For a meal that would please a mariachi musician, why not fix this tangy treat?   ◐   Serves 4 (1 cup)

> 1½ cups (9 ounces) diced Dubuque 97% fat-free ham or any
>   extra-lean ham
> ¼ cup chopped onion
> 1¾ cups (one 14½-ounce can) stewed tomatoes, coarsely chopped
>   and undrained
> 2 teaspoons chili seasoning mix
> 2 cups hot cooked noodles, rinsed and drained

In a large skillet sprayed with olive oil–flavored cooking spray, sauté ham and onion for 5 minutes. Add undrained stewed tomatoes, chili seasoning mix, and noodles. Mix well to combine. Lower heat and simmer for 10 minutes, stirring occasionally.

HINT: 1¾ cups uncooked noodles usually cooks to about 2 cups.

Each serving equals:

HE: 1½ Protein • 1 Vegetable • 1 Bread

212 Calories • 4 gm Fat • 15 gm Protein •
29 gm Carbohydrate • 829 mg Sodium • 3 gm Fiber

DIABETIC: 1½ Starch • 1 Meat • 1 Vegetable

Frankfurter Cabbage Skillet

Cooking "from scratch" may seem like too much trouble, but when you can pick up a bag of prepared coleslaw mix, mix in a few diced fat-free franks, then stir up a sparkling sauce in just moments, you'll discover you can do it. For something that tastes this good, I know you'll find the time!   ❍   Serves 4 (1 cup)

> *4 cups purchased coleslaw mix*
>
> *8 ounces Healthy Choice 97% fat-free frankfurters, diced*
>
> *½ cup (one 2.5-ounce jar) sliced mushrooms, drained*
>
> *1¾ cups (one 15-ounce can) Hunt's Chunky Tomato Sauce*
>
> *1 teaspoon prepared mustard*
>
> *1 tablespoon Brown Sugar Twin*
>
> *¼ teaspoon black pepper*

In a large skillet sprayed with butter-flavored cooking spray, sauté coleslaw mix and frankfurters for 6 to 8 minutes or until cabbage is just tender. Stir in mushrooms and tomato sauce. Add mustard, Brown Sugar Twin, and black pepper. Mix well to combine. Lower heat and simmer for 5 minutes, or until mixture is heated through, stirring occasionally.

HINT: 3½ cups shredded cabbage and ½ cup shredded carrots may be used in place of purchased coleslaw mix.

Each serving equals:

HE: 4 Vegetable • 1⅓ Protein • 1 Optional Calorie

117 Calories • 1 gm Fat • 10 gm Protein •
17 gm Carbohydrate • 1,393 mg Sodium • 2 gm Fiber

DIABETIC: 3 Vegetable • 1 Meat

Apple Dumpling Skillet

I remember watching as my grandma made apple dumplings that filled her kitchen with a sweet fragrance that lingered for hours! Now you can enjoy those scrumptious flavors—and that amazing aroma—in delectably low-fat fashion. If you've never made a dumpling in your life, here's the perfect way to begin!

● Serves 4

> 1 cup unsweetened apple juice
>
> 2 cups water
>
> 1 (4-serving) package JELL-O sugar-free vanilla cook-and-serve pudding mix
>
> 1½ teaspoons apple pie spice☆
>
> 1 cup (2 small) cored, peeled, and chopped cooking apples
>
> ¾ cup Bisquick Reduced Fat Baking Mix
>
> 2 tablespoons Sugar Twin or Sprinkle Sweet
>
> ¼ cup raisins
>
> 2 tablespoons (½ ounce) chopped walnuts
>
> ⅓ cup skim milk

In a large skillet, combine apple juice, water, dry pudding mix, and 1 teaspoon apple pie spice. Stir in apples. Cook over medium heat for 5 to 6 minutes or until apples soften, stirring often. Lower heat. Meanwhile, in a medium bowl, combine baking mix, Sugar Twin, raisins, walnuts, and remaining ½ teaspoon apple pie spice. Add skim milk. Mix well to combine. Drop batter by tablespoonful into hot mixture to form 4 dumplings. Cover and continue cooking for 10 minutes or until dumplings are firm. For each serving, place 1 dumpling into a bowl and spoon about ¾ cup warm apple mixture over top. Serve at once.

HINT: Great served with ¼ cup sugar- and fat-free vanilla ice cream spooned over top, but don't forget to count the few additional calories.

Each serving equals:

HE: 1½ Fruit • 1 Bread • ½ Slider

203 Calories • 3 gm Fat • 3 gm Protein •
41 gm Carbohydrate • 378 mg Sodium • 1 gm Fiber

DIABETIC: 1½ Fruit • 1 Starch

Vermont Bananas Foster

Whoever Mr. Foster was, I thank him for inspiring this truly luscious skillet dessert! It's a little bit tropical, and terrific too. Try it
both ways—over ice cream or on its own!   ☻   Serves 4

¼ *cup (1 ounce) chopped pecans*
⅓ *cup Cary's Sugar Free Maple Syrup*
1 teaspoon rum extract
2 cups (2 medium) sliced bananas

In a large skillet sprayed with butter-flavored cooking spray,
sauté pecans for 2 to 3 minutes. Stir in maple syrup. Bring mixture
to a boil. Add rum extract and bananas. Mix gently to combine.
Continue cooking for 2 to 3 minutes or until bananas are heated
through. Evenly spoon mixture into 4 dessert dishes. Serve at once.

HINT: Wonderful served over sugar- and fat-free vanilla ice
cream, but don't forget to count the additional calories.

Each serving equals:

HE: 1 Fruit • 1 Fat • 13 Optional Calories

133 Calories • 5 gm Fat • 1 gm Protein •
21 gm Carbohydrate • 27 mg Sodium • 2 gm Fiber

DIABETIC: 1 Fruit • 1 Fat

In the Oven

There's something so irresistible about a piping-hot casserole just out of the oven! As you set it on the table, you're sure to hear "Umm-hmm" from everyone seated there!

Oven baking is great for the busy cook because once you set the timer, you can let the oven do its work while you do yours. The actual preparation time is short, and then you're free to leave the kitchen while your dish gets heated through and all crusty and brown on top!

Most of the dishes in this section are prepared in an 8-by-8-inch baking dish and serve four. All you need to do once it's ready to divide it up perfectly is make one cut down the middle in each direction. And you'll see how satisfying that big piece of cozy goodness tastes to every family member, no matter the size of the appetite!

Try to resist the urge to pull the pan out to check it after half the cooking time has elapsed. You'll interrupt the baking cycle and cool off the oven a little from the set temperature. That can produce a soggy, unfinished result.

Cliff just loves to peek into my kitchen each afternoon to see what's baking for dinner that night. I know that with my best healthy recipes for the oven, you're going to bake up a storm!

In the Oven

In the Oven (continued)

Tex-Mex Noodle Bake

Big on taste and texture, big on portion size—yup, it's another of JoAnna's healthy Tex-Mex recipes, ready to earn your approval with every bite! Even though it's prepared without any meat, this hearty dish will satisfy the toughest Texas-sized appetite!

◒ Serves 4

> *10 ounces (one 16-ounce can) pinto beans, rinsed and drained*
>
> *½ cup frozen whole kernel corn*
>
> *¼ cup chunky salsa (mild, medium, or hot)*
>
> *1 cup (one 8-ounce can) Hunt's Tomato Sauce*
>
> *2 teaspoons chili seasoning mix*
>
> *⅛ teaspoon black pepper*
>
> *1½ cups hot cooked noodles, rinsed and drained*
>
> *¾ cup (3 ounces) shredded Kraft reduced-fat Cheddar cheese*

Preheat oven to 350 degrees. Spray an 8-by-8-inch baking dish with olive oil–flavored cooking spray. In a large skillet sprayed with olive oil–flavored cooking spray, combine pinto beans, corn, salsa, tomato sauce, chili seasoning mix, and black pepper. Cook over low heat for 10 to 15 minutes, stirring occasionally. Add noodles. Mix well to combine. Pour mixture into prepared baking dish. Sprinkle Cheddar cheese evenly over top. Bake for 20 to 25 minutes. Place baking dish on a wire rack and let set for 5 minutes. Divide into 4 servings.

HINT: 1¼ cups uncooked noodles usually cooks to about 1½ cups.

Each serving equals:

HE: 2¼ Protein • 1¼ Vegetable • 1 Bread

---

272 Calories • 4 gm Fat • 16 gm Protein •
43 gm Carbohydrate • 597 mg Sodium • 8 gm Fiber

DIABETIC: 2½ Starch • 1½ Meat • 1 Vegetable

Layered Macaroni Casserole

You've heard how doubling your flavor will double your fun? Well, here's a dish that serves up triple-good great taste with its combination of three-count-'em-three delectable cheeses! If two is good, three's gotta be GRRRRREAT! ❂ Serves 4

> 1¾ cups (one 15-ounce can) Hunt's Chunky Tomato Sauce
> ¼ teaspoon dried minced garlic
> 1 teaspoon Italian seasoning
> ¼ teaspoon black pepper
> 2 cups hot cooked macaroni, rinsed and drained
> 1 cup fat-free cottage cheese
> ⅓ cup (1½ ounces) shredded Kraft reduced-fat mozzarella cheese
> ⅓ cup (1½ ounces) shredded Kraft reduced-fat Cheddar cheese
> ¼ cup (¾ ounce) grated Kraft fat-free Parmesan cheese

Preheat oven to 350 degrees. Spray an 8-by-8-inch baking dish with olive oil–flavored cooking spray. In a medium bowl, combine tomato sauce, garlic, Italian seasoning, and black pepper. Spoon about ⅔ cup sauce mixture into prepared baking dish. Layer half of macaroni, half of cottage cheese, and all of mozzarella cheese over top. Spoon half of remaining sauce over mozzarella cheese. Repeat layers with remaining macaroni and cottage cheese. Layer Cheddar cheese over cottage cheese. Stir Parmesan cheese into remaining sauce mixture. Evenly spoon sauce mixture over top. Bake for 35 to 40 minutes. Place baking dish on a wire rack and let set for 2 to 3 minutes. Divide into 4 servings.

HINT: 1⅓ cups uncooked macaroni usually cooks to about 2 cups.

Each serving equals:

HE: 1¾ Protein • 1¾ Vegetable • 1 Bread

223 Calories • 3 gm Fat • 20 gm Protein •
29 gm Carbohydrate • 973 mg Sodium • 1 gm Fiber

DIABETIC: 2 Meat • 2 Vegetable • 1 Starch

Adobe Asparagus Rice Bake

The season for fresh asparagus isn't all that long, so you'll want to make this several times before those scrumptious green stalks disappear from the market! Partnered in pleasure with a creamy sauce and cheese topping, asparagus is, simply, culinary perfection.

○ Serves 4

> 2 cups chopped fresh asparagus
>
> 1 cup hot water
>
> 1 (10¾-ounce) can Healthy Request Tomato Soup
>
> ¼ cup skim milk
>
> 2 teaspoons chili seasoning mix
>
> 2 cups hot cooked rice
>
> ¾ cup (3 ounces) shredded Kraft reduced-fat Cheddar cheese☆

Preheat oven to 350 degrees. Spray an 8-by-8-inch baking dish with butter-flavored cooking spray. In a medium saucepan, combine asparagus and water. Bring mixture to a boil. Cook for 10 minutes or until just tender. Drain. Return asparagus to saucepan. Stir in tomato soup, skim milk, and chili seasoning mix. Add rice and ½ cup Cheddar cheese. Mix well to combine. Pour mixture into prepared baking dish. Sprinkle remaining ¼ cup Cheddar cheese evenly over the top. Bake for 25 to 30 minutes. Place baking dish on a wire rack and let set for 5 minutes. Divide into 4 servings.

HINT: 1⅓ cups uncooked rice usually cooks to about 2 cups.

Each serving equals:

> HE: 1 Vegetable • 1 Bread • 1 Protein • ½ Slider •
> 5 Optional Calories
>
> ---
>
> 217 Calories • 5 gm Fat • 10 gm Protein •
> 33 gm Carbohydrate • 466 mg Sodium • 5 gm Fiber
>
> ---
>
> DIABETIC: 3 Vegetable • 1 Meat • 1 Fat • 1 Starch *or*
> 2 Carbohydrate • 1 Meat

Swiss Broccoli and Noodle Bake

If you've ever tasted broccoli quiche, you know just how delicious a blend of melted Swiss cheese, rich cream, and broccoli can be. Here's a "kissin' cousin" of that popular dish that delivers the same great taste in a noodle casserole. ❍ Serves 6

1 (16-ounce) package frozen chopped broccoli

½ cup finely chopped onion

2¼ cups (3¾ ounce) uncooked medium-width noodles

3 cups hot water

1½ cups (one 12-fluid-ounce can) Carnation Evaporated Skim Milk

3 tablespoons all-purpose flour

6 (¾-ounce) slices Kraft reduced-fat Swiss cheese, shredded

½ cup (one 2.5-ounce jar) sliced mushrooms, drained

¼ teaspoon lemon pepper

Preheat oven to 325 degrees. Spray an 8-by-8-inch baking dish with butter-flavored cooking spray. In a large saucepan, combine broccoli, onion, noodles, and water. Bring mixture to a boil. Cook for 10 minutes or until just tender, stirring occasionally. Drain. In a covered jar, combine evaporated skim milk and flour. Shake well to blend. Pour milk mixture into a medium saucepan sprayed with butter-flavored cooking spray. Add Swiss cheese, mushrooms, and lemon pepper. Mix well to combine. Cook over medium heat for 5 minutes or until mixture thickens and cheese melts, stirring often. Add drained broccoli mixture to sauce mixture. Mix well to combine. Pour mixture into prepared baking dish. Bake for 25 to 30 minutes. Place baking dish on a wire rack and let set for 5 minutes. Divide into 6 servings.

Each serving equals:

HE: 1⅓ Vegetable • 1 Bread • 1 Protein • ½ Skim Milk

181 Calories • 1 gm Fat • 12 gm Protein •
31 gm Carbohydrate • 163 mg Sodium • 4 gm Fiber

DIABETIC: 2 Starch • 1 Vegetable • 1 Meat *or*
2 Carbohydrate • 1 Vegetable • 1 Meat

Tuna-Vegetable Casserole

Here's a tasty mélange of flavors that mingles an abundance of textures in one hearty dish! The crunchy water chestnuts offer a perfect contrast to the creamy mushroom and sour cream sauce.

● Serves 6

> 1 cup (3 ounces) uncooked elbow macaroni
> 1 (16-ounce) package frozen broccoli, cauliflower, and carrot
>   blend
> 3 cups hot water
> 1 (10¾-ounce) can Healthy Request Cream of Mushroom Soup
> 1 cup (one 8-ounce can) sliced water chestnuts, drained, and
>   coarsely chopped
> ¾ cup Land O Lakes no-fat sour cream
> 1 teaspoon Worcestershire sauce
> ½ teaspoon dried minced garlic
> 1 (12-ounce) can white tuna, packed in water, drained and
>   flaked
> ¾ cup (3 ounces) shredded Kraft reduced-fat Cheddar cheese

Preheat oven to 350 degrees. Spray an 8-by-8-inch baking dish with butter-flavored cooking spray. In a large saucepan, combine macaroni, vegetable blend, and water. Bring mixture to a boil. Cook for 10 minutes or just until tender, stirring occasionally. Drain. In a large bowl, combine mushroom soup, water chestnuts, sour cream, Worcestershire sauce, and garlic. Add drained macaroni mixture. Mix well to combine. Stir in tuna and Cheddar cheese. Pour mixture into prepared baking dish. Bake for 30 minutes. Place baking dish on a wire rack and let set for 5 minutes. Divide into 6 servings.

HINT: 1 cup frozen carrots, 1 cup frozen broccoli, and 1 cup frozen cauliflower may be used in place of blended vegetables.

Each serving equals:

HE: 1⅔ Protein • 1 Bread • 1 Vegetable • ½ Slider • 8 Optional Calories

228 Calories • 4 gm Fat • 24 gm Protein •
24 gm Carbohydrate • 591 mg Sodium • 3 gm Fiber

DIABETIC: 2½ Meat • 1 Vegetable • ½ Starch *or*
2½ Meat • 2 Carbohydrate

Creamy Corn and Macaroni Dish

Did you know that cream-style canned corn is actually good for you? Even though it tastes a little bit sinful, it blends beautifully—and healthfully—with macaroni and cheese to please your palate in every way.   ●   Serves 6

> 2 cups hot cooked elbow macaroni, rinsed and drained
> 1 cup (one 8-ounce can) cream-style corn
> 1 (10¾-ounce) can Healthy Request Cream of Mushroom Soup
> ¾ cup (3 ounces) shredded Kraft reduced-fat Cheddar cheese
> 1 teaspoon dried parsley flakes
> ¼ teaspoon black pepper

Preheat oven to 350 degrees. Spray an 8-by-8-inch baking dish with butter-flavored cooking spray. In a medium bowl, combine macaroni, corn, and mushroom soup. Stir in Cheddar cheese, parsley flakes, and black pepper. Pour mixture into prepared baking dish. Bake for 30 minutes. Place baking dish on a wire rack and let set for 5 minutes. Divide into 6 servings.

HINT: 1⅓ cups uncooked macaroni usually cooks to about 2 cups.

Each serving equals:

HE: 1 Bread • ⅔ Protein • ¼ Slider • 8 Optional Calories

159 Calories • 3 gm Fat • 7 gm Protein •
26 gm Carbohydrate • 443 mg Sodium • 1 gm Fiber

DIABETIC: 1½ Starch • ½ Meat

Carrot Fish Bake

It's only a bottle of salad dressing, right? Well, sometimes it is, but in this delightful dish that Ranch dressing becomes a magnificent marinade that transforms plain fish and veggies into a feast.

❍ Serves 4

> *16 ounces white fish, cut into 4 pieces*
> *½ cup Kraft Fat Free Ranch Dressing*
> *2 cups thinly sliced carrots*
> *½ cup chopped onion*
> *1 cup chopped celery*
> *1 teaspoon lemon pepper*

Preheat oven to 350 degrees. Place fish pieces in an 8-by-8-inch baking dish. Spoon 2 tablespoons Ranch dressing over each piece. In a medium bowl, combine carrots, onion, celery, and lemon pepper. Evenly spoon vegetable mixture over fish. Cover and bake 30 minutes. Uncover and continue baking for 10 to 15 minutes or until vegetables are tender and fish flakes easily. Place baking dish on a wire rack and let set for 5 minutes. Divide into 4 servings.

Each serving equals:

HE: 1¾ Vegetable • 1½ Protein • ½ Slider • 10 Optional Calories

173 Calories • 1 gm Fat • 23 gm Protein • 18 gm Carbohydrate • 424 mg Sodium • 2 gm Fiber

DIABETIC: 3 Meat • 2 Vegetable • ½ Starch

Celery Tuna Casserole

We all remember the cozy warm feeling we got when Mom fixed tuna noodle casseroles for winter lunches. Here's a dish I bet any mom would be proud to serve, a version that sparkles with the pizazz of crunchy celery and tasty peas.   ○   Serves 4

> 1 (6-ounce) can white tuna, packed in water, drained and flaked
>
> ½ cup frozen peas
>
> 1 cup finely chopped celery
>
> 1 (10¾-ounce) can Healthy Request Celery Soup
>
> ¼ cup skim milk
>
> 1½ cups cooked noodles, rinsed and drained
>
> ¼ teaspoon black pepper

Preheat oven to 350 degrees. Spray an 8-by-8-inch baking dish with butter-flavored cooking spray. In a large bowl, combine tuna, peas, and celery. Add celery soup, skim milk, noodles, and black pepper. Mix well to combine. Pour mixture into prepared baking dish. Bake for 35 to 40 minutes. Place baking dish on a wire rack and let set for 5 minutes. Divide into 4 servings.

HINT: 1¼ cups uncooked noodles usually cooks to about 1½ cups.

Each serving equals:

HE: 1 Bread • ¾ Protein • ½ Vegetable • ½ Slider •
1 Optional Calorie

191 Calories • 3 gm Fat • 16 gm Protein •
25 gm Carbohydrate • 518 mg Sodium • 3 gm Fiber

DIABETIC: 1½ Starch • 1½ Meat

Italian Oven-Baked Chicken

You could slave over a hot stove for hours, stirring up a sauce that would turn simple baked chicken into a dish that deserves to be called "supreme." Or, you could whip up a quick and luscious version using creamy soup and tangy cheese that will earn you the same applause! ☙ Serves 4

> 16 ounces skinned and boned uncooked chicken breasts, cut into
>   4 pieces
> 1 (10¾-ounce) can Healthy Request Cream of Chicken Soup
> ¼ cup (¾ ounce) grated Kraft fat-free Parmesan cheese
> 1 teaspoon dried parsley flakes
> 1 teaspoon Italian seasoning

Preheat oven to 350 degrees. Spray an 8-by-8-inch baking dish with olive oil–flavored cooking spray. Evenly arrange chicken pieces in prepared baking dish. In a small bowl, combine chicken soup, Parmesan cheese, parsley flakes, and Italian seasoning. Evenly spoon soup mixture over chicken. Cover and bake for 30 minutes. Uncover and continue baking for 15 minutes or until chicken is tender. When serving, evenly spoon sauce over chicken pieces.

Each serving equals:

HE: 3¼ Protein • ½ Slider • 8 Optional Calories

194 Calories • 4 gm Fat • 30 gm Protein •
9 gm Carbohydrate • 498 mg Sodium • 0 gm Fiber

DIABETIC: 3 Meat • ½ Starch

French Glazed Chicken Breasts

For a pretty (and also pretty quick) chicken entree that tastes rich enough for company, give this recipe an audition! It takes just a few simple ingredients—and easily wins you four stars!

☻ Serves 4

> 16 ounces skinned and boned uncooked chicken breast, cut into 4
>   pieces
> ½ cup Kraft Fat Free French Dressing
> 2 teaspoons Dijon mustard
> 1 tablespoon dried onion flakes
> 1 teaspoon dried parsley flakes
> ½ cup (one 2.5-ounce jar) sliced mushrooms, drained

Preheat oven to 375 degrees. Spray an 8-by-8-inch baking dish with butter-flavored cooking spray. Evenly arrange chicken pieces in prepared baking dish. In a small bowl, combine French dressing, mustard, onion flakes, and parsley flakes. Stir in mushrooms. Evenly spoon dressing mixture over chicken pieces. Bake for 30 minutes or until chicken is tender. When serving, evenly spoon sauce over top.

Each serving equals:

HE: 3 Protein • ¼ Vegetable • ½ Slider

220 Calories • 4 gm Fat • 36 gm Protein •
10 gm Carbohydrate • 440 mg Sodium • 1 gm Fiber

DIABETIC: 3 Meat • 1 Starch

Chicken Broccoli Rice Casserole

If you're on a budget, but you want to give your family a succulent, satisfying supper, here's a hearty dish that feeds four on less than half a pound of poultry! One bite, and you'll see that you're not cutting corners when it comes to flavor. ☻ Serves 4

1 (10-ounce) package frozen cut broccoli, thawed

1½ cups hot cooked rice

½ cup chopped onion

1 full cup (6 ounces) diced cooked chicken breast

1 (10¾-ounce) can Healthy Request Cream of Chicken Soup

¼ cup skim milk

¼ teaspoon lemon pepper

Preheat oven to 350 degrees. Spray an 8-by-8-inch baking dish with butter-flavored cooking spray. In a large bowl, combine broccoli, rice, onion, and chicken. Add chicken soup, skim milk, and lemon pepper. Mix gently to combine. Pour mixture into prepared baking dish. Bake for 45 minutes. Place baking dish on a wire rack and let set for 5 minutes. Divide into 4 servings.

HINTS: 1. Thaw broccoli by placing in a colander and rinsing under hot water for one minute.

2. 1 cup uncooked rice usually cooks to about 1½ cups.

3. If you don't have leftovers, purchase a chunk of cooked chicken breast from your local deli.

Each serving equals:

HE: 1½ Protein • 1¼ Vegetable • ¾ Bread • ½ Slider • 16 Optional Calories

211 Calories • 3 gm Fat • 19 gm Protein • 27 gm Carbohydrate • 392 mg Sodium • 3 gm Fiber

DIABETIC: 1½ Meat • 1 Vegetable • 1 Starch

"Grandma's" Turkey and Biscuits

In my family, the foods we remember with pleasure are all wrapped up in happy memories. Here's a recipe for a traditional Sunday lunch that recalls how everything from Grandma's kitchen tasted better when served with love. ● Serves 6

1½ cups (8 ounces) diced cooked turkey breast
1 (10¾-ounce) can Healthy Request Cream of Chicken Soup
1 teaspoon dried onion flakes
1 teaspoon dried parsley flakes
1 cup (one 8-ounce can) sliced carrots, rinsed and drained
1 cup (one 8-ounce can) cut green beans, rinsed and drained
1 (7.5-ounce) can Pillsbury refrigerated buttermilk biscuits
⅓ cup (1½ ounces) shredded Kraft reduced-fat Cheddar cheese

Preheat oven to 375 degrees. Spray an 8-by-8-inch baking dish with butter-flavored cooking spray. In a large bowl, combine turkey, chicken soup, onion flakes, and parsley flakes. Add carrots and green beans. Mix well to combine. Spread mixture into prepared baking dish. Separate biscuits and cut each biscuit into 4 pieces. Evenly sprinkle biscuit pieces over turkey mixture. Sprinkle Cheddar cheese evenly over top. Bake for 20 to 25 minutes or until biscuit pieces are browned. Place baking dish on a wire rack and let set for 5 minutes. Divide into 6 servings.

HINT: If you don't have leftovers, purchase a chunk of cooked turkey breast from your local deli.

Each serving equals:

HE: 1⅔ Protein • 1¼ Bread • ⅔ Vegetable • ¼ Slider • 10 Optional Calories

208 Calories • 4 gm Fat • 18 gm Protein •
25 gm Carbohydrate • 618 mg Sodium • 2 gm Fiber

DIABETIC: 1½ Meat • 1 Starch • 1 Vegetable • ½ Fat

Turkey Casserole Pie

I love the idea of homemade pot pies, but I'm also a busy working woman who isn't likely to prepare this American classic the old-time way. Instead, I invented a speedier version that's perfect for using up holiday leftovers but tastes as if you fussed for hours!

● Serves 6

¾ *cup Bisquick Reduced Fat Baking Mix*

⅔ *cup Carnation Nonfat Dry Milk Powder*

2 eggs or equivalent in egg substitute

1 teaspoon dried parsley flakes

2 teaspoons poultry seasoning

1 cup water

1½ cups (8 ounces) diced cooked turkey breast

1 cup chopped celery

½ cup finely chopped onion

Preheat oven to 375 degrees. Spray a deep-dish 10-inch pie plate with butter-flavored cooking spray. In a large bowl, combine baking mix, dry milk powder, eggs, parsley flakes, poultry seasoning, and water. Mix well using a wire whisk. Stir in turkey, celery, and onion. Pour mixture into prepared pie plate. Bake for 35 to 40 minutes or until knife inserted in center comes out clean. Place pie plate on a wire rack and let set for 5 minutes. Cut into 6 servings.

HINTS: 1. If you don't have leftovers, purchase a chunk of cooked turkey breast from your local deli.

2. Good topped with 1 tablespoon fat-free sour cream, but don't forget to count the few additional calories.

Each serving equals:

HE: 1⅔ Protein • ⅔ Bread • ½ Vegetable • ⅓ Skim Milk

172 Calories • 4 gm Fat • 18 gm Protein •
16 gm Carbohydrate • 274 mg Sodium • 0 gm Fiber

DIABETIC: 2 Meat • 1 Starch

Italian Noodle Casserole

There are certain classic combos I revive in new variations, like this wonderfully flavorful meat and macaroni dish à la Italy! I've kept the calories and fat grams low but jammed in lots of real Italian taste, enough to make your family shout "Bravo!"

● Serves 4

> 8 ounces ground 90% lean turkey or beef
> ½ cup chopped green bell pepper
> ½ cup chopped onion
> 1¾ cups (one 15-ounce can) Hunt's Chunky Tomato Sauce
> 2 teaspoons Italian seasoning
> ¼ cup (¾ ounce) grated Kraft fat-free Parmesan cheese
> ½ cup (one 2.5-ounce jar) sliced mushrooms, drained
> 2 cups hot cooked noodles, rinsed and drained
> ⅓ cup (1½ ounces) shredded Kraft reduced-fat mozzarella
>   cheese

Preheat oven to 350 degrees. Spray an 8-by-8-inch baking dish with olive oil–flavored cooking spray. In a large skillet sprayed with olive oil–flavored cooking spray, brown meat, green pepper, and onion. Stir in tomato sauce, Italian seasoning, and Parmesan cheese. Add mushrooms and noodles. Mix well to combine. Pour mixture into prepared baking dish. Evenly sprinkle mozzarella cheese over top. Bake for 30 minutes. Place baking dish on a wire rack and let set for 5 minutes. Divide into 4 servings.

HINT: 1¾ cups uncooked noodles usually cooks to about 2 cups.

Each serving equals:

HE: 2¼ Protein • 2½ Vegetable • 1 Bread

271 Calories • 7 gm Fat • 21 gm Protein •
31 gm Carbohydrate • 982 mg Sodium • 3 gm Fiber

DIABETIC: 2½ Meat • 2 Vegetable • 1 Starch

Southwest Cabbage Casserole

Cabbage is a terrific base for a meaty baked casserole—rich with good-for-you vitamins and full of texture and taste. Here I've mingled two hearty proteins—the beans and beef or turkey—with tangy seasonings sure to tempt every taste bud!   ☯   Serves 6

3½ cups coarsely shredded cabbage

2 cups hot water

8 ounces ground 90% lean turkey or beef

½ cup chopped onion

½ cup chopped green bell pepper

1¾ cups (one 15-ounce can) Hunt's Chunky Tomato Sauce

10 ounces (one 16-ounce can) red kidney beans, rinsed and
     drained

1 teaspoon dried minced garlic

2 teaspoons chili seasoning mix

¼ cup (¾ ounce) grated Kraft fat-free Parmesan cheese

Preheat oven to 350 degrees. Spray an 8-by-8-inch baking dish with olive oil–flavored cooking spray. In a large saucepan, combine cabbage and water. Bring mixture to a boil. Cook for 10 minutes or just until tender. Drain. Meanwhile, in a large skillet sprayed with olive oil–flavored cooking spray, brown meat, onion, and green pepper. Add tomato sauce, kidney beans, garlic, and chili seasoning mix. Mix well to combine. Stir in drained cabbage. Pour mixture into prepared baking dish. Sprinkle Parmesan cheese evenly over the top. Bake for 25 to 30 minutes. Place baking dish on a wire rack and let set for 5 minutes. Divide into 6 servings.

Each serving equals:

HE: 2⅔ Vegetable • 2 Protein

139 Calories • 3 gm Fat • 12 gm Protein •
16 gm Carbohydrate • 557 mg Sodium • 4 gm Fiber

DIABETIC: 1½ Meat • 1 Vegetable • ½ Starch

Mexican Pizza Strata

"Strata" means layers, and this easy supper dish takes just a little time to assemble, then puffs up so moist and good! You need to allow for the hour of baking time, but you don't have to watch this as it bakes—it knows just what to do!   ☻   Serves 4

>   8 ounces ground 90% lean turkey or beef
>
>   2 teaspoons chili seasoning mix
>
>   2 cups chunky salsa (mild, medium, or hot)
>
>   1 cup (one 8-ounce can) Hunt's Tomato Sauce
>
>   8 slices reduced-calorie white bread
>
>   ¾ cup (3 ounces) shredded Kraft reduced-fat Cheddar cheese☆
>
>   2 eggs or equivalent in egg substitute
>
>   2 cups skim milk
>
>   1 teaspoon dried parsley flakes

Preheat oven to 350 degrees. Spray a 9-by-9-inch cake pan with olive oil–flavored cooking spray. In a large skillet sprayed with olive oil–flavored cooking spray, brown meat. Stir in chili seasoning mix, salsa, and tomato sauce. Lower heat and simmer for 5 minutes, stirring occasionally. Remove from heat. Place 4 slices of bread in prepared cake pan. Sprinkle half of Cheddar cheese over bread. Spoon half of meat mixture over cheese. Repeat layers. In a medium bowl, beat eggs with a wire whisk. Add skim milk and parsley flakes. Mix well to combine. Pour milk mixture evenly over top. Bake for 60 minutes or until edges are lightly browned and center is firm. Place cake pan on a wire rack and let set for 5 minutes. Cut into 4 servings.

HINTS: 1.   If you can find Wonder Sourdough Fat Free Bread, it works great.

2.   Strata may be covered and refrigerated up to 24 hours before baking.

Each serving equals:

HE: 3 Protein (½ limited) • 2 Vegetable • 1 Bread •
½ Skim Milk

296 Calories • 8 gm Fat • 30 gm Protein •
26 gm Carbohydrate • 872 mg Sodium • 1 gm Fiber

DIABETIC: 3 Meat • 2 Vegetable • 1 Starch

Layered Kraut Casserole

Here's another flavorful and easy dish you simply "build," then bake! Sauerkraut is one of those foods that delivers so much tangy taste, but not a lot of calories. You'll be pleased and even a little amazed how all the ingredients in this dish work together.

○ Serves 6

> 16 ounces ground 90% lean turkey or beef
> 2 cups (one 16-ounce can) sauerkraut, well drained
> ½ cup chopped onion
> 1 cup (3 ounces) uncooked regular rice
> 1¾ cups (one 15-ounce can) Hunt's Chunky Tomato Sauce
> ½ cup water
> ¼ teaspoon black pepper
> 2 tablespoons Brown Sugar Twin

Preheat oven to 350 degrees. Spray an 8-by-8-inch baking dish with butter-flavored cooking spray. In a large skillet sprayed with butter-flavored cooking spray, brown meat. Meanwhile, layer sauerkraut in prepared baking dish. Layer onion and uncooked rice over sauerkraut. Sprinkle browned meat over top. In a medium bowl, combine tomato sauce, water, black pepper, and Brown Sugar Twin. Pour sauce mixture evenly over top. Cover and bake for 60 minutes. Uncover and continue baking for 15 minutes, or until rice is tender. Place baking dish on a wire rack and let set for 5 minutes. Divide into 6 servings.

Each serving equals:

> HE: 2 Protein • 2 Vegetable • ½ Bread •
> 2 Optional Calories

---

170 Calories • 6 gm Fat • 15 gm Protein •
14 gm Carbohydrate • 961 mg Sodium • 2 gm Fiber

DIABETIC: 2 Meat • 1 Vegetable • 1 Starch

Meat 'n' Potatoes Casserole

If your family relishes the hearty flavor of a meal that's clearly meat and potatoes, why not try this fast and easy dish that bakes up oh-so-luscious and lovely on your table? Not only that, but a substantial serving supplies just under 200 calories! It's gotta be magic!

● Serves 6

> 16 ounces ground 90% lean turkey or beef
> 3 cups (15 ounces) peeled, sliced raw potatoes
> ¾ cup chopped onion
> 1 (10¾-ounce) can Healthy Request Cream of Chicken Soup
> ⅛ teaspoon black pepper

Preheat oven to 350 degrees. Spray an 8-by-8-inch baking dish with butter-flavored cooking spray. In a large skillet sprayed with butter-flavored cooking spray, brown meat. Add potatoes, onion, chicken soup, and black pepper. Mix well to combine. Pour mixture into prepared baking dish. Cover and bake for 45 minutes. Uncover and continue baking for 15 minutes or until potatoes are tender. Divide into 6 servings.

Each serving equals:

HE: 2 Protein • ½ Bread • ¼ Vegetable • ¼ Slider • 10 Optional Calories

199 Calories • 7 gm Fat • 16 gm Protein • 18 gm Carbohydrate • 297 mg Sodium • 0 gm Fiber

DIABETIC: 2 Meat • 1 Starch

Baked Salisbury Steak and Rice

Oh, the aroma that will emerge from your kitchen while this man-pleasing dish bakes beautifully! You'll feel like a whiz of a chef when the soup, ketchup, and Worcestershire sauce brew up into a taste worthy of a party! ○ Serves 4

1½ cups cold cooked rice

1 teaspoon dried parsley flakes

8 ounces ground 90% lean turkey or beef

7 small fat-free saltine crackers, made into crumbs

1 egg or equivalent in egg substitute

½ cup chopped onion or 2 tablespoons dried onion flakes

⅛ teaspoon black pepper

1 (10¾-ounce) can Healthy Request Cream of Mushroom Soup

2 tablespoons Worcestershire sauce

3 tablespoons Heinz Light Harvest or Healthy Choice ketchup

½ cup water

Preheat oven to 350 degrees. Spray an 8-by-8-inch baking dish with butter-flavored cooking spray. Layer rice and parsley flakes in prepared baking dish. In a large bowl, combine meat, cracker crumbs, egg, onion, and black pepper. Mix well to combine. Form mixture into 4 patties and place patties in a large skillet sprayed with butter-flavored cooking spray. Brown patties for 3 to 4 minutes on both sides. Arrange browned patties over rice. In a medium bowl, combine mushroom soup, Worcestershire sauce, ketchup, and water. Pour soup mixture evenly over meat patties. Cover and bake for 30 minutes. Uncover and continue baking for 15 minutes. Place baking dish on a wire rack and let set for 5 minutes. Divide into 4 servings.

Each serving equals:

HE: 1¾ Protein (¼ limited) • 1 Bread • ¼ Vegetable • ½ Slider • 13 Optional Calories

223 Calories • 7 gm Fat • 14 gm Protein • 26 gm Carbohydrate • 513 mg Sodium • 1 gm Fiber

DIABETIC: 2 Meat • 1½ Starch

Hamburger Milk Gravy Cabbage Casserole

Here's another classic milk gravy dish created with my son Tommy in mind. This one invites the crunch of coleslaw to dance alongside the meat and creamy gravy. The cheese and bread crumb topping made this dish one of his "Top Ten List"! ◐ Serves 4

> 4 cups purchased coleslaw mix
>
> 2 cups hot water
>
> 8 ounces ground 90% lean turkey or beef
>
> 1½ cups (one 12-fluid-ounce can) Carnation Evaporated Skim Milk
>
> 3 tablespoons all-purpose flour
>
> ½ cup (one 2.5-ounce jar) sliced mushrooms, drained
>
> ⅛ teaspoon black pepper
>
> 3 tablespoons (¾ ounce) dried fine bread crumbs
>
> ⅓ cup (1½ ounces) shredded Kraft reduced-fat Cheddar cheese
>
> 1 teaspoon dried parsley flakes

Preheat oven to 350 degrees. Spray an 8-by-8-inch baking dish with butter-flavored cooking spray. In a large saucepan, combine coleslaw mix and water. Bring mixture to a boil. Cook for 10 minutes or just until tender. Drain. Meanwhile, in a large skillet sprayed with butter-flavored cooking spray, brown meat. In a covered jar, combine evaporated skim milk and flour. Shake well to blend. Stir milk mixture into browned meat. Continue cooking for 5 minutes or until mixture starts to thicken, stirring often. Add mushrooms and black pepper. Mix well to combine. Stir in drained coleslaw mix. Pour mixture into prepared baking dish. In a small bowl, combine bread crumbs, Cheddar cheese, and parsley flakes. Sprinkle crumb mixture evenly over top. Bake for 25 to 30 minutes. Place baking dish on a wire rack and let set for 5 minutes. Divide into 4 servings.

HINT: 3½ cups shredded cabbage and ½ cup shredded carrots
may be used in place of purchased coleslaw mix.

Each serving equals:

HE: 1½ Bread • 1¼ Protein • ½ Skim Milk • ½ Slider •
1 Optional Calorie

255 Calories • 7 gm Fat • 23 gm Protein •
25 gm Carbohydrate • 469 mg Sodium • 3 gm Fiber

DIABETIC: 2 Meat • 1 Skim Milk • 1 Free Vegetable •
½ Starch

Sassy Kraut and Pork

Here's a great dish for a family get-together, full of irresistible flavors and so positively pretty when it emerges from the oven all golden brown! Because it serves eight, you've got plenty for a large group, but if you're only cooking tonight for you and your family—hurray, there'll be leftovers that you can freeze! ● Serves 8

> 1½ cups (8 ounces) diced lean cooked roast pork
> 1¾ cups (one 14½-ounce can) Frank's Bavarian-style
>   sauerkraut, well drained
> 1¾ cups (one 14½-ounce can) stewed tomatoes, undrained
> 2 cups canned (one 16-ounce can) cut green beans, rinsed and
>   drained
> ½ cup chopped onion
> 1 cup (1½ ounces) Pepperidge Farm unseasoned dry bread cubes
> ¾ cup (3 ounces) shredded Kraft reduced-fat Cheddar cheese

Preheat oven to 350 degrees. Spray a 9-by-13-inch baking dish with butter-flavored cooking spray. In a large bowl, combine pork, sauerkraut, undrained stewed tomatoes, green beans, and onion. Add dry bread cubes. Mix well to combine until bread cubes soften. Evenly spread mixture into prepared baking dish. Bake for 30 minutes. Sprinkle Cheddar cheese evenly over top. Continue baking for 10 minutes or until cheese melts. Place baking dish on a wire rack and let set for 5 minutes. Divide into 8 servings.

HINT: If you don't have leftovers, purchase a chunk of cooked roast pork from your local deli.

Each serving equals:

HE: 1½ Protein • 1½ Vegetable • ¼ Bread

---

152 Calories • 4 gm Fat • 12 gm Protein •
17 gm Carbohydrate • 613 mg Sodium • 3 gm Fiber

DIABETIC: 1½ Meat • 1 Vegetable • ½ Starch

Throw Together Pork Dish

Are you having one of those nights when you come home exhausted and just want to "throw together" something easy for dinner? Why not mix up this short list of tasty ingredients, slide your casserole dish into the oven, and go enjoy a hot bath while it bubbles away? You'll feel better, and dinner will be delicious.   ☻   Serves 6

1 full cup (6 ounces) diced lean cooked roast pork

¼ cup chopped onion

½ cup (one 2.5-ounce jar) sliced mushrooms, drained

2¼ cups hot cooked noodles, rinsed and drained

1 cup (one 8-ounce can) cream-style corn

1 (10¾-ounce) can Healthy Request Cream of Mushroom Soup

⅓ cup (1½ ounces) shredded Kraft reduced-fat Cheddar cheese

7 small fat-free saltine crackers, made into crumbs

1 teaspoon dried parsley flakes

Preheat oven to 350 degrees. Spray an 8-by-8-inch baking dish with butter-flavored cooking spray. In a large bowl, combine pork, onion, mushrooms, and noodles. Stir in corn and mushroom soup. Add Cheddar cheese. Mix gently to combine. Pour mixture into prepared baking dish. In a small bowl, combine cracker crumbs and parsley flakes. Evenly sprinkle crumb mixture over top. Lightly spray top with butter-flavored cooking spray. Bake for 45 minutes. Place baking dish on a wire rack and let set for 5 minutes. Divide into 6 servings.

HINT: 2 cups uncooked noodles usually cooks to about 2¼ cups.

Each serving equals:

HE: 1¼ Bread • 1⅓ Protein • ¼ Vegetable • ¼ Slider • 8 Optional Calories

196 Calories • 4 gm Fat • 10 gm Protein • 30 gm Carbohydrate • 709 mg Sodium • 1 gm Fiber

DIABETIC: 1½ Starch • 1½ Meat

Creamed Chipped Beef Casserole

If you've never enjoyed this traditional creamy meat dish before, why not give this midwestern classic a try? In the original version, it's usually served on top of toast, but mine goes that one better: it bakes up thick and fragrant and full of hearty taste!

● Serves 6

2 (2.5-ounce) packages Hormel Dried Beef, shredded
¼ cup finely chopped onion
2 cups skim milk
3 tablespoons all-purpose flour
1 (8-ounce) package Philadelphia fat-free cream cheese
½ cup (one 2.5-ounce jar) sliced mushrooms, drained
¾ cup (3 ounces) shredded Kraft reduced-fat Cheddar cheese
2 teaspoons dried parsley flakes
2 cups hot cooked noodles, rinsed and drained
½ cup frozen peas

Preheat oven to 350 degrees. Spray an 8-by-8-inch baking dish with butter-flavored cooking spray. In a large skillet sprayed with butter-flavored cooking spray, sauté dried beef and onion for 5 minutes. In a covered jar, combine skim milk and flour. Shake well to blend. Add milk mixture to beef mixture. Mix well to combine. Stir in cream cheese. Continue cooking for 5 minutes or until mixture starts to thicken. Stir in mushrooms, Cheddar cheese, and parsley flakes. Add noodles and peas. Mix well to combine. Pour mixture into prepared baking dish. Bake for 25 to 30 minutes. Place baking dish on a wire rack and let set for 5 minutes. Divide into 6 servings.

HINT: 1¾ cups uncooked noodles usually cooks to about 2 cups.

Each serving equals:

HE: 2 Protein • 1 Bread • ⅓ Skim Milk • ¼ Vegetable • 10 Optional Calories

241 Calories • 5 gm Fat • 20 gm Protein • 29 gm Carbohydrate • 632 mg Sodium • 2 gm Fiber

DIABETIC: 2 Meat • 2 Starch

Italian Pork and Spaghetti Bake

Here's a tasty pasta casserole brimming over with flavor and fun! Those bits of pimiento, olive, and bacon peeking out promise a fast and easy feast with every bite, and the preparation couldn't be simpler. I bet you'll agree with me that varying the ground meat in your casseroles keeps life interesting!   ○   Serves 4

8 ounces ground 90% lean pork

½ cup chopped onion

1¾ cups (one 15-ounce can) Hunt's Chunky Tomato Sauce

¼ cup chopped pimientos

½ cup (one 2.5-ounce jar) sliced mushrooms, drained

¼ cup (1 ounce) sliced ripe olives

2 cups hot cooked spaghetti, rinsed and drained

¼ cup (¾ ounce) grated Kraft fat-free Parmesan cheese

2 tablespoons Hormel Bacon Bits

Preheat oven to 350 degrees. Spray an 8-by-8-inch baking dish with olive oil–flavored cooking spray. In a large skillet sprayed with olive oil–flavored cooking spray, brown meat and onion. Stir in tomato sauce and pimientos. Add mushrooms, olives, and spaghetti. Mix well to combine. Spread mixture in prepared baking dish. Evenly sprinkle Parmesan cheese and bacon bits over top. Bake for 30 minutes. Place baking dish on a wire rack and let set for 5 minutes. Divide into 4 servings.

HINT: 1½ cups uncooked spaghetti usually cooks to about 2 cups.

Each serving equals:

HE: 2¼ Vegetable • 1¾ Protein • 1 Bread • ¼ Fat • 13 Optional Calories

261 Calories • 5 gm Fat • 22 gm Protein • 32 gm Carbohydrate • 902 mg Sodium • 3 gm Fiber

DIABETIC: 2 Vegetable • 2 Meat • 1½ Starch

Corn-Frankfurter Bake

Ever have one of those weekend days when everyone is so busy, you barely see one another? Well, here's a simple casserole that will call every family member to the table just by its homey aroma! The mustard gives the corn and franks that wonderful taste of the ballpark.   ○   Serves 4

> 2 cups (one 16-ounce can) cream-style corn
>
> 6 tablespoons (1½ ounces) dried fine bread crumbs
>
> 2 teaspoons dried onion flakes
>
> ½ teaspoon prepared mustard
>
> 1 teaspoon dried parsley flakes
>
> ⅛ teaspoon black pepper
>
> 8 ounces Healthy Choice 97% fat-free frankfurters, diced

Preheat oven to 350 degrees. Spray an 8-by-8-inch baking dish with butter-flavored cooking spray. In a medium bowl, combine corn, bread crumbs, onion flakes, mustard, parsley flakes, and black pepper. Add frankfurters. Mix well to combine. Pour mixture into prepared baking dish. Bake for 30 minutes. Place baking dish on a wire rack and let set for 5 minutes. Divide into 4 servings.

Each serving equals:

HE: 1½ Bread • 1⅓ Protein

149 Calories • 1 gm Fat • 7 gm Protein •
28 gm Carbohydrate • 684 mg Sodium • 1 gm Fiber

DIABETIC: 1½ Starch • 1 Meat

Noodle, Kraut, and Frankfurter Casserole

Here's a great family supper perfect for sitting down together to watch football on TV—or maybe the Rose Bowl Parade! It's tangy and satisfying, so full of your kids' favorite tastes they'll actually quiet down while they're eating it! ● Serves 4

> 8 ounces Healthy Choice 97% fat-free frankfurters, diced
> 1¾ cups (one 14½-ounce can) Frank's Bavarian-style
>   sauerkraut, well drained
> ¼ cup chopped onion
> 1 (10¾-ounce) can Healthy Request Tomato Soup
> 2 cups hot cooked noodles, rinsed and drained
> ¾ cup (3 ounces) shredded Kraft reduced-fat Cheddar cheese

Preheat oven to 375 degrees. Spray an 8-by-8-inch baking dish with butter-flavored cooking spray. Place frankfurters in prepared baking dish. In a medium bowl, combine sauerkraut, onion, and tomato soup. Layer half the sauerkraut mixture over frankfurters. Cover with noodles. Evenly arrange Cheddar cheese over noodles. Top with remaining sauerkraut mixture. Bake for 30 minutes. Place baking dish on a wire rack and let set for 5 minutes. Divide into 4 servings.

HINTS: 1. If you can't find Bavarian sauerkraut, use regular sauerkraut, ½ teaspoon caraway seeds, and 1 teaspoon Brown Sugar Twin.

2. 1 full cup of diced 97% fat-free ham may be used in place of frankfurters.

3. 1¾ cups uncooked noodles usually cooks to about 2 cups.

Each serving equals:

HE: 2⅓ Protein • 1 Bread • 1 Vegetable • ½ Slider •
5 Optional Calories

252 Calories • 4 gm Fat • 13 gm Protein •
41 gm Carbohydrate • 1,387 mg Sodium • 7 gm Fiber

DIABETIC: 2 Meat • 2 Starch • 2 Vegetable

Polish Sausage and Rice Scallop

My family loves sausage, so now that we can find tasty versions that are nearly fat-free, we can enjoy it much more often! I've stirred lots of our favorite flavors into this old-fashioned baked dish, which cooks up so cheesy and creamy, they'll rise from their chairs to cheer you! ❍ Serves 6

> 2 cups hot cooked rice
> 1 cup frozen peas
> 8 ounces Healthy Choice 97% fat-free Kielbasa sausage, sliced
>   into ¼-inch pieces
> ¾ cup (3 ounces) shredded Kraft reduced-fat Cheddar cheese
> 1 tablespoon dried parsley flakes
> ½ teaspoon lemon pepper
> 1 (10¾-ounce) can Healthy Request Cream of Mushroom Soup

Preheat oven to 350 degrees. Spray an 8-by-8-inch baking dish with butter-flavored cooking spray. In a large bowl, combine rice, peas, sausage, and Cheddar cheese. Add parsley flakes, lemon pepper, and mushroom soup. Mix well to combine. Pour mixture into prepared baking dish. Bake for 30 minutes. Place baking dish on a wire rack and let set for 2 to 3 minutes. Divide into 6 servings.

HINTS: 1.   1⅓ cups uncooked rice usually cooks to about 2 cups.

           2.   Healthy Choice frankfurters may be used in place of Kielbasa sausage.

Each serving equals:

HE: 1½ Protein • 1 Bread • ¼ Slider •
11 Optional Calories

184 Calories • 4 gm Fat • 14 gm Protein •
23 gm Carbohydrate • 632 mg Sodium • 2 gm Fiber

DIABETIC: 1½ Meat • 1½ Starch

Maui Ham Casserole

Ham is one of those meats that makes fast friends with fruit, so I created an island-inspired dish that celebrates that tasty relationship! The topping is made even more heavenly by the addition of a few chopped pecans. ● Serves 6

> 1½ cups cold cooked rice
>
> 1½ cups (9 ounces) diced Dubuque 97% fat-free ham or any extra-lean ham
>
> 1 cup (one 8-ounce can) crushed pineapple, packed in fruit juice, undrained
>
> 1 (10¾-ounce) can Healthy Request Cream of Mushroom Soup
>
> 1 teaspoon dried parsley flakes
>
> ¼ teaspoon black pepper
>
> 3 tablespoons purchased graham cracker crumbs or 3 (2½-inch) squares made into crumbs
>
> 2 tablespoons (½ ounce) chopped pecans

Preheat oven to 350 degrees. Spray an 8-by-8-inch baking dish with butter-flavored cooking spray. In a large bowl, combine rice, ham, and undrained pineapple. Add mushroom soup, parsley flakes, and black pepper. Mix well to combine. Pour mixture into prepared baking dish. In a small bowl, combine graham cracker crumbs and pecans. Evenly sprinkle crumb mixture over top. Bake for 45 minutes. Place baking dish on a wire rack and let set for 5 minutes. Divide into 6 servings.

HINT: 1 cup uncooked rice usually cooks to about 1½ cups.

Each serving equals:

HE: 1 Protein • ⅔ Bread • ⅓ Fruit • ⅓ Fat • ¼ Slider • 8 Optional Calories

162 Calories • 4 gm Fat • 8 gm Protein •
23 gm Carbohydrate • 595 mg Sodium • 0 gm Fiber

DIABETIC: 1 Meat • 1 Starch • ½ Fruit • ½ Fat

Cabbage and Ham Casserole

With my Healthy Exchanges recipes, you'll become such a whiz at whipping up casseroles, you're bound to be invited to every potluck in town! This popular one stirs up quickly, bakes to a golden glory in just a half hour, and might just win you a blue ribbon!

○ Serves 6

> 3 cups shredded cabbage
>
> 1 cup shredded carrots
>
> 1½ cups (3 ounces) uncooked noodles
>
> 1½ cups hot water
>
> 1½ cups (one 12-fluid-ounce can) Carnation Evaporated Skim Milk
>
> 3 tablespoons all-purpose flour
>
> ⅛ teaspoon black pepper
>
> ¾ cup (3 ounces) shredded Kraft reduced-fat Cheddar cheese
>
> ½ cup (one 2.5-ounce jar) sliced mushrooms, drained
>
> 1 full cup (6 ounces) diced Dubuque 97% fat-free ham or any extra-lean ham
>
> 3 tablespoons (¾ ounce) dried fine bread crumbs

Preheat oven to 350 degrees. Spray an 8-by-8-inch baking dish with butter-flavored cooking spray. In a large saucepan, combine cabbage, carrots, noodles, and water. Bring mixture to a boil. Cook for 10 to 12 minutes or until vegetables are tender, stirring occasionally. Drain. Meanwhile, in a covered jar, combine evaporated skim milk, flour, and black pepper. Shake well to blend. Pour milk mixture into same saucepan, now sprayed with butter-flavored cooking spray. Add Cheddar cheese, mushrooms, and ham. Mix well to combine. Continue cooking, stirring often, until mixture thickens and cheese melts. Add drained cabbage mixture. Mix gently to combine. Pour mixture into prepared baking dish. Evenly sprinkle bread crumbs over top. Lightly spray top with butter-flavored cooking spray. Bake for 25 to 30 minutes. Place baking dish on a wire rack and let set for 5 minutes. Divide into 6 servings.

Each serving equals:

HE: 1½ Vegetable • 1⅓ Protein • 1 Bread •
½ Skim Milk

---

216 Calories • 4 gm Fat • 17 gm Protein •
28 gm Carbohydrate • 521 mg Sodium • 2 gm Fiber

DIABETIC: 1½ Meat • 1 Vegetable • 1 Starch • ½ Skim Milk
or 2 Carbohydrate • 1½ Meat

Ham Salad Casserole

The ingredients in this cozy dish might seem to belong in a cool summer salad, but why not forget about the season and just slide them into a hot oven? What emerges only a short time later will please everyone at your table!   ●   Serves 4

1 full cup (6 ounces) finely diced Dubuque 97% fat-free ham or
* any extra-lean ham*
1 cup finely diced celery
¼ cup (1 ounce) sliced green olives
2 tablespoons canned chopped pimientos
2 tablespoons finely chopped onion
½ cup Kraft fat-free mayonnaise
⅛ teaspoon black pepper
1 tablespoon lemon juice
2 teaspoons prepared mustard
2 hard-boiled eggs, diced
7 small fat-free saltine crackers, crushed
2 teaspoons dried parsley flakes

Preheat oven to 400 degrees. Spray an 8-by-8-inch baking dish with butter-flavored cooking spray. In a large bowl, combine ham, celery, olives, pimientos, and onion. In a small bowl, combine mayonnaise, black pepper, lemon juice, and mustard. Add mayonnaise mixture to ham mixture. Mix well to combine. Gently fold in eggs. Pour mixture into prepared baking dish. In a small bowl, combine cracker crumbs and parsley flakes. Sprinkle crumb mixture evenly over ham mixture. Lightly spray top with butter-flavored cooking spray. Bake for 25 to 30 minutes. Place baking dish on a wire rack and let set for 5 minutes. Divide into 4 servings.

HINT: If you want the look and feel of eggs without the cholesterol, toss out the yolk and dice the white.

Each serving equals:

HE: 1½ Protein (½ limited) • ½ Vegetable • ¼ Bread • ¼ Fat • ¼ Slider

133 Calories • 5 gm Fat • 11 gm Protein • 11 gm Carbohydrate • 872 mg Sodium • 0 gm Fiber

DIABETIC: 2 Meat • ½ Starch

Country Style Ham and Noodles

One of my favorite culinary secrets (and one I'm happy to share with you) blends evaporated skim milk and a bit of flour to create a perfect creamy sauce base! When stirred into this luscious ham and noodles concoction, it thickens up quickly and bakes up delectably rich! ● Serves 4

1½ cups (one 12-fluid-ounce can) Carnation Evaporated Skim
    Milk

3 tablespoons all-purpose flour

2 teaspoons prepared mustard

½ cup (one 2.5-ounce jar) sliced mushrooms, drained

¼ teaspoon black pepper

1½ cups hot cooked noodles, rinsed and drained

½ cup frozen peas

1 full cup (6 ounces) finely diced Dubuque 97% fat free ham or
    any extra-lean ham

¼ cup (¾ ounce) grated Kraft fat-free Parmesan cheese

Preheat oven to 350 degrees. Spray an 8-by-8-inch baking dish with butter-flavored cooking spray. In a covered jar, combine evaporated skim milk and flour. Shake well to blend. Pour milk mixture into a large saucepan sprayed with butter-flavored cooking spray. Cook over medium heat for 5 minutes or until mixture starts to thicken, stirring often. Add mustard, mushrooms, and black pepper. Mix well to combine. Stir in noodles, peas, and ham. Pour mixture into prepared baking dish. Evenly sprinkle Parmesan cheese over top. Bake for 25 to 30 minutes. Place baking dish on a wire rack and let set for 5 minutes. Divide into 4 servings.

HINT: 1¼ cups uncooked noodles usually cooks to about 1½
        cups.

Each serving equals:

HE: 1¼ Protein • 1¼ Bread • ¾ Skim Milk •
¼ Vegetable

259 Calories • 3 gm Fat • 21 gm Protein •
37 gm Carbohydrate • 660 mg Sodium • 3 gm Fiber

DIABETIC: 1½ Starch • 1 Meat • 1 Skim Milk

Baked Beans and Ham

This may be one of the easiest casseroles I ever dreamed up, and if you've got to be away on a visit, I know that the most inexperienced cook in your household could mix this up in a minute! It's a true tangy man-pleaser! ☻ Serves 6

> 2 (16-ounce) cans pork and beans, undrained
> 2 tablespoons hot dog relish
> 1 teaspoon dried minced onion
> ½ cup (3 ounces) diced Dubuque 97% fat-free ham or any extra-lean ham
> 2 tablespoons Brown Sugar Twin
> 2 tablespoons Sugar Twin or Sprinkle Sweet

Preheat oven to 350 degrees. Spray an 8-by-8-inch baking dish with butter-flavored cooking spray. In a medium saucepan, combine pork and beans, hot dog relish, and onion. Bring mixture to a boil. Remove from heat. Stir in ham, Brown Sugar Twin, and Sugar Twin. Pour mixture into prepared baking dish. Bake for 30 to 35 minutes. Place pan on a wire rack and let set for 5 minutes. Divide into 6 servings.

HINT: 2 tablespoons dill pickle relish and 1 teaspoon prepared mustard may be used in place of hot dog relish.

Each serving equals:

HE: 2 Protein • 9 Optional Calories

---

121 Calories • 1 gm Fat • 7 gm Protein •
21 gm Carbohydrate • 565 mg Sodium • 4 gm Fiber

DIABETIC: 1½ Starch • 1 Meat

Fruit Monkey Bread

Where did the name "monkey bread" come from for this dish composed of balls of tasty dough? Rumors mention the Far East, but wherever it originated, I've made it even better with the addition of your favorite spreadable fruit. You'll find it's fun to eat, too, as you pull apart this tasty, pretty bread!   ☉ Serves 10 (2 each)

½ teaspoon apple pie spice
¼ cup Sugar Twin or Sprinkle Sweet
2 (7.5-ounce) packages Pillsbury refrigerated buttermilk biscuits
⅓ cup spreadable fruit spread (any flavor)

Preheat oven to 375 degrees. Spray a bundt pan with butter-flavored cooking spray. In a small bowl, combine apple pie spice and Sugar Twin. Separate biscuits. Flatten each biscuit into a 3-inch circle. Place ½ teaspoon fruit spread in center of each biscuit. Wrap each biscuit to form a ball. Roll biscuit balls in apple pie spice mixture. Arrange 10 balls in bundt pan, seam side up. Lightly spray top with butter-flavored cooking spray. Arrange remaining 10 balls seam side down between balls of first layer. Sprinkle any remaining apple pie spice mixture evenly over top. Lightly spray top with butter-flavored cooking spray. Bake for 20 minutes or until golden brown. Place pan on a wire rack and let set for 5 minutes. Turn upside down onto a serving plate and pat bread out of pan. Lightly spray with butter-flavored cooking spray. Allow to cool for 10 minutes. Break balls apart when serving.

Each serving equals:

HE: 1½ Bread • ½ Fruit • 5 Optional Calories

---

129 Calories • 1 gm Fat • 3 gm Protein •
27 gm Carbohydrate • 374 mg Sodium • 2 gm Fiber

DIABETIC: 2 Starch or Carbohydrate

"Old Time"
Baked Noodle Pudding

Lots of families enjoy a fruited noodle pudding recipe brought over by their ancestors from Eastern Europe. My version is so filled with nuts and fruits, it's bound to become a New World classic—and perhaps a new family tradition at your house! ● Serves 6

> 1 cup (one 8-ounce can) crushed pineapple, packed in fruit juice, drained, and ⅓ cup liquid reserved
>
> 1 cup (one 8-ounce can) sliced peaches, packed in fruit juice, drained, and ⅓ cup liquid reserved
>
> 1 cup water
>
> 1 (4-serving) package JELL-O sugar-free vanilla cook-and-serve pudding mix
>
> ⅔ cup Carnation Nonfat Dry Milk Powder
>
> 1 teaspoon vanilla extract
>
> 2 tablespoons Brown Sugar Twin
>
> ½ teaspoon apple pie spice
>
> ¼ cup raisins
>
> ⅓ cup (1½ ounces) chopped walnuts
>
> 2 cups cold cooked noodles, rinsed and drained

Preheat oven to 350 degrees. Spray an 8-by-8-inch baking dish with butter-flavored cooking spray. In a medium saucepan, combine reserved fruit liquid, water, dry pudding mix, and dry milk powder. Mix well using a wire whisk. Cook over medium heat, stirring constantly, until mixture thickens and starts to boil. Remove from heat. Stir in vanilla extract, Brown Sugar Twin, and apple pie spice. Add pineapple, peaches, raisins, walnuts, and noodles. Mix well to combine. Pour mixture into prepared baking dish. Bake for 30 minutes. Cut into 6 servings. Good warm or cold.

HINT: 1¾ cups uncooked noodles usually cooks to about 2 cups.

Each serving equals:

HE: 1 Fruit • ⅔ Bread • ½ Fat • ¼ Protein •
¼ Skim Milk • 15 Optional Calories

225 Calories • 5 gm Fat • 7 gm Protein •
38 gm Carbohydrate • 125 mg Sodium • 2 gm Fiber

DIABETIC: 1½ Starch • 1 Fruit • 1 Fat *or*
2½ Carbohydrate • 1 Fat

Quick Cherry Cobbler

Here's a sweet dessert that's sure to convince your family and friends that you've been taking secret baking lessons! (Well, your secret's safe with me, anyway . . .) What could be more deliciously American than a hot cherry "pie"? ☻ Serves 6

> 1 (4-serving) package JELL-O sugar-free vanilla cook-and-serve
>   pudding mix
> 1 (4-serving) package JELL-O sugar-free cherry gelatin
> 2 cups (one 16-ounce can) tart red cherries, packed in water,
>   undrained
> ½ cup water
> 1 (7.5-ounce) can Pillsbury refrigerated buttermilk biscuits
> ¼ teaspoon ground cinnamon
> 1 tablespoon Sugar Twin or Sprinkle Sweet

Preheat oven to 425 degrees. Spray an 8-by-8-inch baking dish with butter-flavored cooking spray. In a medium saucepan, combine dry pudding mix, dry gelatin, undrained cherries, and water. Cook over medium heat, stirring constantly, until mixture thickens and starts to boil, being careful not to crush cherries. Remove from heat. Spoon mixture into prepared baking dish. Separate biscuits and cut each biscuit into 4 pieces. Evenly sprinkle biscuit pieces over cherry mixture. Lightly spray top with butter-flavored cooking spray. In a small bowl, combine cinnamon and Sugar Twin. Evenly sprinkle cinnamon mixture over top. Bake for 13 to 16 minutes or until top is golden brown. Place baking dish on a wire rack and let set for 5 minutes. Cut into 6 servings. Good warm or cold.

Each serving equals:

HE: 1¼ Bread • ⅔ Fruit • ¼ Slider • 1 Optional Calorie

137 Calories • 1 gm Fat • 4 gm Protein •
28 gm Carbohydrate • 439 mg Sodium • 2 gm Fiber

DIABETIC: 1 Starch • 1 Fruit *or*
2 Carbohydrate

Easy Pear Crisp

What's the difference between a cobbler and a crisp? They're both filled to the brim with scrumptious fruit, but a crisp tops off all that sweet taste with a nutty-crumbly topping that might just be the best part!   ● Serves 4

> 2 cups (one 16-ounce can) pears, packed in fruit juice, drained, and ½ cup liquid reserved
> ¾ cup purchased graham cracker crumbs or 12 (2½-inch) squares made into crumbs ☆
> 2 tablespoons (½ ounce) chopped pecans
> 2 tablespoons Sugar Twin or Sprinkle Sweet
> ½ teaspoon apple pie spice

Preheat oven to 375 degrees. Spray an 8-by-8-inch baking dish with butter-flavored cooking spray. Coarsely chop pears. Reserve 2 tablespoons graham cracker crumbs. In a medium bowl, combine chopped pears, reserved pear liquid, and remaining 10 tablespoons graham cracker crumbs. Mix gently to combine. Spoon mixture into prepared baking dish. In a small bowl, combine reserved graham cracker crumbs, pecans, Sugar Twin, and apple pie spice. Evenly sprinkle crumb mixture over top. Bake for 18 to 20 minutes. Good warm or cold.

HINT: Good served with 1 tablespoon Cool Whip Lite, but don't forget to count the few additional calories.

Each serving equals:

HE: 1 Fruit • 1 Bread • ½ Fat • 3 Optional Calories

193 Calories • 5 gm Fat • 2 gm Protein •
35 gm Carbohydrate • 143 mg Sodium • 2 gm Fiber

DIABETIC: 1 Fruit • 1 Starch • 1 Fat or
2 Carbohydrate • 1 Fat

In the Slow Cooker

If you used to own a slow cooker but found you didn't use it much, you probably sold it at one of your garage sales! Well, it's time to track down another one. When these were first introduced more than twenty years ago, busy people liked the idea but weren't always sure how thoroughly these all-day pots cooked a meal.

I'm happy to say that the slow cooker has stood the test of time, and now many cooks who let their slow cookers gather dust in the basement or attic have brought back these golden oldies with gusto!

Here are some terrific ideas for getting these cookers to do what they do best—blend a variety of ingredients into a rich tapestry of taste. They're perfect for cooking up stews and soups, and they make wonderful party entrees that can be served straight from the pot.

If you've never owned a slow cooker, why not pick one up at your church rummage sale or a local secondhand shop and give it a whirl? (Or spring for a brand-new one the next time they're on sale!) I think you'll be pleased to welcome its special help to your kitchen!

In the Slow Cooker

Cabbage Chili Soup

Just imagine coming home after a long, hard day at the office and lifting the top off a slow cooker filled to the brim with this flavorful soup! The chili spices are just tangy enough to tickle your taste buds, and the rich broth created by the cabbage mingling for hours with those tomatoes will win your heart.

O Serves 4 (1½ cups)

> 3 cups coarsely chopped cabbage
>
> 1 cup chopped onion
>
> 3 cups Healthy Choice tomato juice or any reduced-sodium
>   tomato juice
>
> 1 (10¾-ounce) can Healthy Request Tomato Soup
>
> 10 ounces (one 16-ounce can) kidney beans, rinsed and drained
>
> 2 teaspoons chili seasoning mix

In a slow cooker, combine cabbage, onion, tomato juice, and tomato soup. Add kidney beans and chili seasoning mix. Mix well to combine. Cover and cook on LOW for 6 to 8 hours. Mix well before serving.

Each serving equals:

HE: 3½ Vegetable • 1¼ Protein • ½ Slider •
5 Optional Calories

---

178 Calories • 2 gm Fat • 7 gm Protein •
33 gm Carbohydrate • 320 mg Sodium • 11 gm Fiber

DIABETIC: 3 Vegetable • 1 Starch • 1 Meat *or*
2 Carbohydrate • 1 Meat

"Roasted" Veggie Trio Pot

It's just an easy blend of carrots, onions, and potatoes, but what a magnificent dish it becomes when the beef broth soaks into the veggies and transforms their flavor into something very special!

⊙ Serves 4 (1 full cup)

> 3 cups (15 ounces) sliced raw potatoes
> 3 cups sliced carrots
> ½ cup chopped onion
> 1¾ cups (one 15-ounce can) Swanson Beef Broth

In a slow cooker, combine potatoes, carrots, and onion. Pour beef broth evenly over top. Cover and cook on HIGH for 4 to 6 hours. Mix well before serving.

Each serving equals:

HE: 1¾ Vegetable • ¾ Bread • 9 Optional Calories

128 Calories • 0 gm Fat • 4 gm Protein •
28 gm Carbohydrate • 412 mg Sodium • 2 gm Fiber

DIABETIC: 2 Vegetable • 1 Starch *or*
2 Carbohydrate

Hot German Potato Salad

Warm potato salad is a wonderful choice for a cold-weather buffet, and this recipe makes that treat deliciously easy! Aren't you surprised to find tapioca in this list of ingredients? Trust me, it works!

❍ Serves 8 (¾ cup)

> 6 cups (30 ounces) sliced raw potatoes
> 1 cup chopped onion
> 1 cup chopped celery
> 1 cup water
> ¼ cup cider vinegar
> ¼ cup Sugar Twin or Sprinkle Sweet
> 2 tablespoons quick-cooking tapioca
> ¼ teaspoon black pepper
> 2 teaspoons dried parsley flakes
> ¼ cup Hormel Bacon Bits

In a slow cooker, combine potatoes, onion, and celery. In a medium bowl, combine water, vinegar, Sugar Twin, tapioca, black pepper, and parsley flakes. Pour mixture over potato mixture. Mix well to combine. Cover and cook on LOW for 8 hours. Stir in bacon bits. Serve warm.

Each serving equals:

HE: ¾ Bread • ½ Vegetable • ¼ Slider •
3 Optional Calories

125 Calories • 1 gm Fat • 4 gm Protein •
25 gm Carbohydrate • 189 mg Sodium • 0 gm Fiber

DIABETIC: 1½ Starch

Party Time Beans

If you've got the time, I've got the beans! This hearty version is a true "Cliff-pleaser" with its tangy-sweet taste and bits of tasty ham. After just a few bites, wait and see if your tongue starts to tango!

⊙ Serves 6 (1 full cup)

> 30 ounces (three 16-ounce cans) great northern beans, rinsed and drained
>
> ½ cup chopped onion
>
> 1 full cup (6 ounces) finely diced Dubuque 97% fat-free ham or any extra-lean ham
>
> ½ cup chunky salsa (mild, medium, or hot)
>
> 1¾ cups (one 15-ounce can) Hunt's Chunky Tomato Sauce
>
> 2 tablespoons Sugar Twin or Sprinkle Sweet
>
> 2 tablespoons Brown Sugar Twin
>
> ¼ teaspoon black pepper

In a slow cooker, combine great northern beans, onion, and ham. Add salsa, tomato sauce, Sugar Twin, Brown Sugar Twin, and black pepper. Mix well to combine. Cover and cook on LOW for 6 to 8 hours. Mix well before serving.

Each serving equals:

HE: 3 Protein • 1½ Vegetable • 13 Optional Calories

217 Calories • 1 gm Fat • 16 gm Protein •
36 gm Carbohydrate • 724 mg Sodium • 8 gm Fiber

DIABETIC: 2 Starch • 1½ Vegetable • 1 Meat

Farmhouse Macaroni and Cheese

It's rich and creamy, stirs up fast, then cooks oh-so-slowly and delectably! I've created lots of mac and cheese recipes, but this one just sizzles with cozy goodness. Let it simmer while you're trimming the tree or out Christmas shopping, then savor it slowly surrounded by those you love best! ☺ Serves 6 (1 cup)

> *3 cups cooked elbow macaroni, rinsed and drained*
> *2 tablespoons Hormel Bacon Bits*
> *¼ cup chopped onion*
> *1¾ cups (one 14½-ounce can) stewed tomatoes, undrained*
> *1½ cups (6 ounces) shredded Kraft reduced-fat Cheddar cheese*
> *1 (10¾-ounce) can Healthy Request Cream of Mushroom Soup*

In a slow cooker, combine macaroni, bacon bits, onion, undrained stewed tomatoes, and Cheddar cheese. Pour mushroom soup over top. Mix well to combine. Cover and cook on LOW for 6 to 8 hours. Mix well before serving.

HINT: 2 cups uncooked macaroni usually cooks to about 3 cups.

Each serving equals:

HE: 1⅓ Protein • 1 Bread • ⅔ Vegetable • ¼ Slider • 18 Optional Calories

230 Calories • 6 gm Fat • 13 gm Protein • 31 gm Carbohydrate • 665 mg Sodium • 2 gm Fiber

DIABETIC: 1½ Starch • 1 Meat • 1 Vegetable *or* 2 Carbohydrate • 1 Meat

Scallop Potato-Tomato Pot

The longer this dish cooks, the more irresistible it gets! These creamy potatoes are a little bit of heaven in one big pot, and everyone will dig in noisily as soon as they're served.

○ Serves 6 (1 cup)

6 cups (20 ounces) frozen shredded hash browns
2 cups (one 16-ounce can) cut green beans, rinsed and drained
¼ cup finely chopped onion
1 teaspoon dried parsley flakes
1 (10¾-ounce) can Healthy Request Cream of Celery Soup
1¾ cups (one 14½-ounce can) stewed tomatoes, undrained

In a slow cooker, combine hash browns, green beans, and onion. In a medium bowl, combine parsley flakes, celery soup, and undrained stewed tomatoes. Add soup mixture to potato mixture. Mix well to combine. Cover and cook on LOW for 6 to 8 hours. Mix well before serving.

HINT: Mr. Dell's frozen shredded potatoes are a good choice *or* raw shredded potatoes may be used in place of frozen potatoes.

Each serving equals:

HE: 1⅓ Vegetable • ⅔ Bread • ¼ Slider •
8 Optional Calories

238 Calories • 2 gm Fat • 6 gm Protein •
49 gm Carbohydrate • 447 mg Sodium • 5 gm Fiber

DIABETIC: 2 Vegetable • 1 Starch *or*
2 Carbohydrate

Lemon Baked Chicken

What starts out tart becomes a luscious and lovely sauce for the chicken you've baked for hours in your cooker. You've never tasted chicken this tender before, and you'll be dazzled by the look of this dish as much as the taste! ☻ Serves 4

> 16 ounces skinned and boned uncooked chicken breast, cut into 4
>   pieces
> 1 lemon
> 1 teaspoon lemon pepper
> 1 teaspoon paprika

Place chicken pieces in a slow cooker. Squeeze juice of half a lemon over chicken. Sprinkle lemon pepper and paprika over top. Cut remaining lemon half into thin slices. Arrange slices around chicken. Cover and cook on HIGH for 4 hours.

Each serving equals:

HE: 3 Protein

180 Calories • 4 gm Fat • 35 gm Protein •
1 gm Carbohydrate • 84 mg Sodium • 0 gm Fiber

DIABETIC: 3 Meat

Ranch Hand Limas

Beans have always tasted best when stewed over a slow fire, and now you can get that taste with a slow-cooked dish sure to please the hungriest ranch hand—or husband! Those spices transform an everyday dish into one you'd be proud to serve to special friends.

○ Serves 6 (1 cup)

8 ounces ground 90% lean turkey or beef
½ cup finely chopped onion
20 ounces (two 16-ounce cans) butter beans, rinsed and drained
1¾ cups (one 15-ounce can) Hunt's Chunky Tomato Sauce
2 tablespoons Brown Sugar Twin
½ teaspoon poultry seasoning
¼ teaspoon ground sage
¼ teaspoon garlic powder

In a large skillet sprayed with butter-flavored cooking spray, brown meat and onion. Spoon browned meat into a slow cooker. Add butter beans, tomato sauce, Brown Sugar Twin, poultry seasoning, sage, and garlic powder. Mix well to combine. Cover and cook on LOW for 6 to 8 hours. Mix well before serving.

HINT: Butter beans are sometimes labeled large lima beans.

Each serving equals:

HE: 2⅔ Protein • 1⅓ Vegetable • 2 Optional Calories

131 Calories • 3 gm Fat • 11 gm Protein •
15 gm Carbohydrate • 505 mg Sodium • 4 gm Fiber

DIABETIC: 1 Meat • 1 Starch • 1 Vegetable

Supper Time Stew

Here's a classic slow-cooker recipe—a beefy-tomato-y stew that just gets better and better as it bubbles along slowly! The Italian seasoning makes a simple dish sparkle with the tangy taste of the Mediterranean. ❍ Serves 6 (1¼ cups)

16 ounces ground 90% lean turkey or beef

3 cups (15 ounces) sliced raw potatoes

1½ cups chopped celery

2 cups sliced carrots

1 cup chopped onion

1½ cups frozen peas

1¾ cups (one 15-ounce can) Hunt's Chunky Tomato Sauce

2 teaspoons Italian seasoning

In a large skillet sprayed with butter-flavored cooking spray, brown meat. Meanwhile, in a slow cooker, combine potatoes, celery, carrots, onion, and peas. Spoon browned meat over vegetables. In a small bowl, combine tomato sauce and Italian seasoning. Evenly pour sauce over meat. Cover and cook on LOW for 6 to 8 hours. Mix well before serving.

Each serving equals:

HE: 2⅔ Vegetable • 2 Protein • 1 Bread

234 Calories • 6 gm Fat • 19 gm Protein •
26 gm Carbohydrate • 592 mg Sodium • 3 gm Fiber

DIABETIC: 2 Meat • 2 Vegetable • 1½ Starch

Heartland Scallop

Meat and potatoes, corn and creamy soup—if those aren't the perfect ingredients to win a man's heart, then I don't know what they could be! The flavors in this one pot dish are as midwestern as they come—and simply spectacular. ☻ Serves 6 (1 full cup)

16 ounces ground 90% lean turkey or beef
½ cup chopped onion
1 cup (one 8-ounce can) cream-style corn
½ cup (one 2.5-ounce jar) sliced mushrooms, drained
1 (10¾-ounce) can Healthy Request Cream of Chicken Soup
Scant 6 cups (20 ounces) shredded frozen hash brown potatoes

In a large skillet sprayed with butter-flavored cooking spray, brown meat and onion. Spoon browned-meat mixture into a slow cooker. Add corn, mushrooms, and chicken soup. Mix well to combine. Stir in potatoes. Cover and cook on LOW for 6 to 8 hours. Mix well before serving.

HINTS: Mr. Dell's frozen shredded potatoes are a good choice *or* raw shredded potatoes may be used in place of frozen potatoes.

Each serving equals:

HE: 2 Protein • 1 Bread • ⅓ Vegetable • ¼ Slider • 8 Optional Calories

255 Calories • 7 gm Fat • 17 gm Protein • 31 gm Carbohydrate • 490 mg Sodium • 2 gm Fiber

DIABETIC: 2 Starch • 2 Meat

Veggie and Ham Macaroni and Cheese

Macaroni and cheese is an American classic, one that every family tends to treasure. By adding the color and flavors of vegetables to this popular favorite, I've increased its good nutrition; and by stirring in some diced lean ham, I've added to its special flavor. Couldn't you eat macaroni and cheese every night for a week? Cliff surely could! ○ Serves 6 (1 cup)

1½ cups (one 12-fluid-ounce can) Carnation Evaporated Skim Milk

3 tablespoons all-purpose flour

1½ cups (6 ounces) shredded Kraft reduced-fat Cheddar cheese

2 teaspoons prepared mustard

¼ teaspoon black pepper

2½ cups hot cooked elbow macaroni, rinsed and drained

1 full cup (6 ounces) diced Dubuque 97% fat-free ham or any extra-lean ham

1 cup (one 8-ounce can) cut green beans, rinsed and drained

1 cup (one 8-ounce can) sliced carrots, rinsed and drained

In a covered jar, combine evaporated skim milk and flour. Shake well to blend. Pour milk mixture into a large skillet sprayed with butter-flavored cooking spray. Cook over medium heat for 5 minutes or until mixture starts to thicken, stirring often. Stir in Cheddar cheese, mustard, and black pepper. Pour mixture into a slow cooker. Add macaroni, ham, green beans, and carrots. Mix well to combine. Cover and cook on LOW for 4 to 6 hours. Mix well before serving.

HINT: 1⅔ cups uncooked macaroni usually cooks to about 2½ cups.

Each serving equals:

HE: 2 Protein • 1 Bread • ⅔ Vegetable • ½ Skim Milk

249 Calories • 5 gm Fat • 21 gm Protein •
30 gm Carbohydrate • 544 mg Sodium • 2 gm Fiber

DIABETIC: 2 Meat • 2 Starch • ½ Vegetable

Down on the Farm Bean Pot

Tangy-sweet and simmered slowly, this beans-and-ham combo brings out the best in all its ingredients! You'll be intrigued by how a spicier-than-usual salsa is tamed just a bit by some added sweetness—and a cooking time that lasts and lasts.

● Serves 6 (1 cup)

4 cups (two 16-ounce cans) cut green beans, rinsed and drained, and ½ cup liquid reserved

20 ounces (two 16-ounce cans) great northern beans, rinsed and drained

½ cup (3 ounces) finely diced Dubuque 97% fat-free ham or any extra-lean ham

½ cup chopped onion

½ cup chunky salsa (mild, medium, or hot)

2 tablespoons Brown Sugar Twin

In a slow cooker, combine green beans, great northern beans, ham, and reserved liquid. Add onion, salsa, and Brown Sugar Twin. Mix well to combine. Cover and cook on LOW for 6 to 8 hours. Mix well before serving.

Each serving equals:

HE: 2 Protein • 1⅔ Vegetable • 2 Optional Calories

157 Calories • 1 gm Fat • 11 gm Protein •
26 gm Carbohydrate • 197 mg Sodium • 7 gm Fiber

DIABETIC: 2 Vegetable • 1 Meat • 1 Starch

Index of Recipes

I want to hear from you . . .

Besides my family, the love of my life is creating "common folk" healthy recipes and solving everyday cooking questions in *The Healthy Exchanges Way*. Everyone who uses my recipes is considered part of the Healthy Exchanges Family, so please write to me if you have any questions, comments, or suggestions. I will do my best to answer. With your support, I'll continue to stir up even more recipes and cooking tips for the Family in the years to come.

Write to: JoAnna M. Lund
c/o Healthy Exchanges, Inc.
P.O. Box 124
DeWitt, IA 52742

If you prefer, you can call me at 1-319-659-8234, fax me at 1-319-659-2126, or contact me via E-mail by writing to HealthyJo @aol.com.

Now that you've seen *One Pot Favorites,* why not order *The Healthy Exchanges Food Newsletter?*

If you enjoyed the recipes in this cookbook and would like to cook up even more of these "common folk" healthy dishes, you may want to subscribe to *The Healthy Exchanges Food Newsletter.*

This monthly 12-page newsletter contains 30-plus new recipes *every month* in such columns as:

- Reader Exchange
- Reader Requests
- Recipe Makeover
- Micro Corner
- Dinner for Two
- Crock Pot Luck
- Meatless Main Dishes
- Rise & Shine
- Our Small World
- Brown Bagging It
- Snack Attack
- Side Dishes
- Main Dishes
- Desserts

In addition to all the recipes, other regular features include:
- The Editor's Motivational Corner
- Dining Out Question & Answer
- Cooking Question & Answer
- New Product Alert
- Success Profiles of Winners in the Losing Game
- Exercise Advice from a Cardiac Rehab Specialist
- Nutrition Advice from a Registered Dietitian
- Positive Thought for the Month

Just as in this cookbook, all *Healthy Exchanges Food Newsletter* recipes are calculated in three distinct ways: 1) Weight Loss Choices, 2) Calories with Fat and Fiber Grams, and 3) Diabetic Exchanges.

The cost for a one-year (12-issue) subscription with a special Healthy Exchanges 3-ring binder to store the newsletters in is $27.50. To order, simply complete the form and mail to us *or* call our toll-free number and pay with your VISA or MasterCard.

_____ Yes, I want to subscribe to *The Healthy Exchanges Food Newsletter.* $27.50 Yearly Subscription Cost............................... $_____

_____ Foreign orders please add $6.00 for money exchange and extra postage.................. $_____

_____ I'm not sure, so please send me a sample copy at $2.50..................................... $_____

Please make check payable to HEALTHY EXCHANGES or pay by VISA/MasterCard

CARD NUMBER:_____ EXPIRATION DATE:_____

SIGNATURE:_____

Signature required for all credit card orders.

Or order toll-free, using your credit card, at 1-800-766-8961

NAME: _____

ADDRESS: _____

CITY _____ STATE _____ ZIP _____

TELEPHONE: ( ) _____

If additional orders for the newsletter are to be sent to an address other than the one listed above, please use a separate sheet and attach to this form.

MAIL TO: **HEALTHY EXCHANGES**
P.O. BOX 124
DeWitt, IA 52742-0124

1-800-766-8961 For Customer Orders
1-319-659-8234 For Customer Service

Thank you for your order, and for choosing to become a part of the Healthy Exchanges Family!

About the Author

JoAnna M. Lund is the author of *Healthy Exchanges Cookbook; HELP: Healthy Exchanges Lifetime Plan*; and *The Diabetic's Healthy Exchanges Cookbook*. She has been profiled in national and local publications, including *People, The New York Times, Forbes*, and *The National Enquirer*, and has appeared on hundreds of radio and television shows. A popular speaker with weight loss, cardiac, and diabetic support groups, she can be seen weekly on public television with her show *Help Yourself with JoAnna Lund.*